ONE STEP(PE) AT A TIME

by Lori (Martin) Potts Zimmerman

Copyright ©2025 by Lori (Martin) Potts Zimmerman (Higher Ground Books & Media). All rights reserved. No part of this publication may be reproduced in any form, stored in a retrieval system, or transmitted in any form, or by any means (electronic, mechanical, photocopying, recording or otherwise) without prior permission by the copyright owner and the publisher of this book.

Scripture taken from the HOLY BIBLE, NEW INTERNATIONAL VERSION®. NIV®. Copyright © 1973, 1978, 1984 by International Bible Society. Used by permission of Zondervan. All rights reserved worldwide.

Higher Ground Books & Media
Springfield, OH 45504
www.highergroundbooksandmedia.com

Because of the dynamic nature of the Internet, any web addresses or links contained in this book may have changed since publication and may no longer be valid. The views expressed in the work are solely those of the author and do not necessarily reflect the views of the publisher, and the publisher hereby disclaims any responsibility for them.

Any people depicted in stock imagery are being used for illustrative purposes only.

ISBN (Paperback): 978-1-955368-94-0

Printed in the United States of America 2025

One Step(pe) at a Time

FOREWORD

Lori attended a church which I later was privileged to pastor: A pretty, red-brick church in Pennsylvania Dutch country. I came to know, and enjoy, the friendship of Lori and her husband David. I appreciated their passion for leading lost souls to the Lord. My wife Julie and I followed their pastoral ministry and finally their family's mission to Kazakhstan. I had to admire their courage (which I wasn't sure I, myself had).

A few years ago, Julie and I returned to that church in New Holland, PA for a visit. During the service of worship, the praise group came forward. Lori sang a solo, accompanying herself on the guitar. She sang, not to entertain, but to praise God!

Suddenly I was enraptured as the message, and the music filled my soul. Then this happened. I heard the Lord speaking to me, not with an audible voice, but rather something like a thought transference, as if He were saying to me, "Tell Lori to write her story. Encourage her to share her thoughts, feelings, and insights. Ask her, on My behalf, to put all of this in writing so that other hearts may be quickened and other lives transformed." I had the strong feeling that the Lord wasn't making a suggestion. It was something He was instructing me to do.

So, after the worship service, I approached Lori and told her what the Lord wanted me to say to her. Admittedly, that's a lot to drop into someone's lap. I added that I knew of a publishing company called Higher Ground Books & Media. Its owner/publisher, Rebecca Benston, made it her life's work to offer a platform for authors with a message. If someone had a story to tell, Rebecca would make sure they could tell it.

As the months passed, the Holy Spirit would nudge me to contact Lori. I would call and pester her to keep working on her autobiographical narrative. I even shared how she might arrange her chapters.

The book you are now holding is her response. Lori teaches us what it means to be obedient to the Lord. When He wants us to follow His plan, He generally doesn't reveal to us the whole plan, start to finish, instead, He beckons us to follow Him one step at a time. That way, each step of the way, we learn to trust Him.

"For we walk by faith, not by sight." 2 Corinthians 5:7 (KJV)

John Henry Newman, a Roman Catholic Cardinal, wrote a hymn titled, "Lead, Kindly Light." In the first verse he wrote:

> "Lead, kindly Light, amid the encircling gloom,
> Lead thou me on!
> The night is dark, and I am far from home;
> Lead thou me on!
> Keep thou my feet; I do not ask to see
> The distant scene; one step enough for me."

Rev. Jerry C. Crossley
August 2025

Table of Contents

Chapter One My Family	Page 9
Chapter Two Growing Up with Hard Work and Play	Page 15
Chapter Three Growing Up in the Church Believing in Jesus	Page 23
Chapter Four Meeting David and Our Lives Together Ministry with David and Adoration Ministries	Page 27
Chapter Five The Writing of Gave Me You - A Song for Lori	Page 37
Chapter Six Preparing for Full-Time Ministry	Page 39
Chapter Seven Amanda Born Into Our Family	Page 43
Chapter Eight A Move to New London Church A Work Trip to Kazakhstan	Page 47
Chapter Nine One Step(pe) at a Time Toward Kazakhstan	Page 55
Chapter Ten Living in Kazakhstan	Page 63
Chapter Eleven David Forever with the Lord	Page 81
Chapter Twelve Where Can Worship Take Place?	Page 85

Chapter Thirteen   Page 87
New Steps Forward

Chapter Fourteen   Page 97
Talk about Steps Forward?

Chapter Fifteen   Page 103
Closing
God Shows Up and Glorifies Himself

Addendum   Page 107
List of Original Songs

Chapter One
My Family
Beulah & Richard Martin, My Mom & Dad

Beulah Grace (Petersheim) Martin, my mom. Mom was born into a family of 8 children, and she is number 4 (3 boys and 5 girls). Only one sister is living as of this writing. Mom had great love for God, for her husband and her 10 children: 2 boys and 8 girls within 14 years, her 21 grandchildren, 30 great grandchildren, and 1 great, great grandchild. My siblings' names in age order from oldest to youngest are: Larry, Linda, Merle, Marcia, Audrey, Peggy, Barbara, Annette, Lori, and Sally. Marcia is in heaven with Jesus. I am number 9. Mom loved our church, Evangelical United Methodist Church in New Holland, Pennsylvania (EUM) and the children she taught there for over 30 years.

One time while my mom was working, she had a visit by twins that she had in her Sunday school class. They gave her some pictures they had made for her, while they had been visiting with their grandmother. Their grandmother asked them for whom they were drawing their pictures. Their response was to give the pictures to their Sunday school teacher because she loved them.

My mom began to work full-time outside our home after the youngest started school (I was 8 years old at the time). She taught Sunday School, raised us kids and took care of our large garden with vegetables and over 20 fruit and nut trees which provided our food for the winter. I always referred to our garden as a "truck patch" because of its size. It was land that ran behind our two neighbors' houses and was deeper than it was wide. Over the years, many people would ask my mom, "How did you raise 10 children and everything that goes with that?" Mom's response was always, "With God's help, love, and hard work, I just did what needed to get done; along with the help of the older children taking care of the younger children."

After my youngest sister started school, mom bought a Wilton Home Cake Decorating Course. She taught herself to decorate cakes and then walked across the street to Achenbach's Pastry Shop (a favorite Lancaster County Bakery) and asked if she could work. She was hired. However, she did not start working until we had a family meeting. I remember mom and dad getting us kids together to tell us that mom was going to start working outside the home. They wanted us to know that some days mom would not be home when we got home from school. They also wanted to know that we were willing to take on some responsibilities without her being right there. For example, we needed to do our homework when we got home from school. Also, someone would need to get dinner ready, and the table needed to be set for dinner. As my older sisters started getting jobs after school, I think I was about 12 years old or so when I started making dinner. After I got home from school, I would drop off my books in the house and check to see if mom left any messages about dinner. Then, I would go across the street to Achenbach's where mom was working and talk to her about what to make for dinner. Not too long ago I came across a small scrap piece of paper that I wrote on mom's instructions for making tomato soup for the family based on her homemade 2-quart canned tomato juice. I can't believe I still have that scrap piece of paper tucked inside my cookbook.

    Mom was very artistic and could free-handedly draw anything we kids, or anyone else would ask her to draw on the top of a cake. Many people would give her pictures of trucks, cars or houses or any other items they wanted her to draw on their special cake. She decorated all our 16th Birthday party cakes. We only had a very big birthday party with friends invited for our 16th birthday. Otherwise, we would have cake and ice cream just with the family for our other birthdays. She decorated all of our bridal shower cakes and most of my siblings' and my wedding cakes. She prepared almost all of the food for our wedding receptions; she even made a lot of our flower arrangements for our weddings too. This all while she was still working full-time and caring for her family. I get really tired just thinking about all that she was able to do.

    Mom was also a seamstress and made a lot of dresses for her 8 girls. Often there was a new dress at Christmas or Easter and many times all 8 dresses were the same or similar. However, we didn't always have new clothes. There were many times I remember sitting down with a bag of clothes that someone had given to our family. We would go through it to see what each of us would be able to wear. We also wore loads of hand-me-downs. One year she even made jackets and ties for the boys and daddy. She made many of my sisters' bridesmaid dresses and at least one wedding dress. When she was much older, she made several outfits for herself.

    When we were younger, our Christmas gifts were put in a brown paper grocery bag. Mom and dad always had a plan so they could always treat us fairly. From my perspective as number 9 in the family, there were specific gifts that we would receive depending on our age so we could always count on that one very specific gift along with the normal pajamas, underwear, socks and maybe an outfit. For example, at a certain age, our Christmas gift would be a clock radio or at a certain age, our Christmas gift would be a wristwatch. It was fun to see what they would pick out for us.

As we got older, mom would often make items for Christmas gifts for us kids and then the grandkids as they came along. She would start right after Christmas making her plan and began to make the items. Very rarely did mom and dad just buy Christmas gifts. She made vests, aprons, bookmarks, book covers, tree ornaments out of felt, quilted lap blankets, quilted casserole covers, quilted book (and music) bags. She made baby quilts for each first grandchild born in each family. In the later part of her life, she quilted extra baby blankets for new members of our family yet to be born.

I can't sew at all. In fact, in high school, she helped me finish a dress I had to make for homemaker's class. I would never have been able to pass that class without her help.

I remember coming home from school, when mom was home, and telling her all about my day. She always understood, even when I didn't understand my own feelings and what was happening. Oh, those teenage years were so difficult. I remember she often cried with me.

When we wanted to invite friends over, mom would always say the more the merrier. Without question, mom was always open to feeding and taking care of us and all of our friends.

I have no doubt that I had the absolute best mom in the world! It was just before Christmas in 2017 when mom at the age of 90 went to her home with Jesus in heaven.

M. (Mahlon) Richard Martin, my dad. Daddy was born into a family of 10 children, 5 boys and 5 girls. Daddy was number 8. Daddy was a very hard worker and took great care of his family. He worked full-time, helped just about anyone that asked for his help, and made many wooden items for our home and the church. One item he made was a bank that looks just like a church for my mom's children's Sunday school class. He also sold greeting cards, helped mom cut corn off the cob until the wee hours of the night, (because we couldn't be trusted with the knife and do it the right way!!), and he always had some project going on making cupboards or bookshelves. He made countless picture frames and used his lathe to make many useful items and gifts. He made cutting boards in the shape of a pig as gifts and rolling pins for his kids' wedding gifts. He could make just about anything you could think of out of wood. Sometimes mom would buy items and daddy would try to figure out how to duplicate them out of wood.

One item he made, which I think is one of his earliest projects, was a Chinese Checkerboard. I believe he was 14 years old when he carved all the holes for the marbles and made a very fine Chinese Checkerboard. Daddy would play baseball, volleyball, and badminton with us. Often, we all played lawn croquet on a Sunday afternoon. One year he bought lawn darts for us to play.

My oldest sister said one time, that we grew up in 2 different families from the oldest children to the younger children. I think she was right, because there are things we did with daddy that I don't think he did with the older children.

There were at least a couple of times that he was called upon to help his brother on the family farm. He would get up at the crack of dawn…go milk the cows… take the milk to the milk house… and then go to his full-time job. He would finish his job and then go milk the cows again… take the milk to the milk house… plow a field… bring the tractor to our house and plow our garden... go to bed and then do it all over again the next day.

I have no doubt that I had the absolute best dad in the world! It was just before Father's Day, in 2018 that daddy at the age of 91 went to his home with Jesus in heaven within six months of when mom died.

My father had a nickname for me (actually there were a few nicknames). I kind of had forgotten about those nicknames until I was talking with a couple of my sisters after mom & daddy moved into a care facility and we were going through their house to get it ready to be sold. I don't remember my father having any nicknames for any of my siblings which is very interesting to me now. He may have, but I don't recall any. I loved it when I heard my father's voice call my nickname.

When we were in language school to learn Russian, as we began our classes, the whole class was given Russian names. My name was "Lara." One of my teachers called me a name which I didn't like. That teacher called me "Laritchka." Every time he called out my name for an answer, I cringed and completely messed up any answers I gave. It totally threw me. The ending, "itchka" is a diminutive form. Every time I heard that name, Laritchka, my thoughts went to something like "you're just a little girl" and "you are never gonna learn this language" "you are just simply little Lara." I thought he didn't like me very much and I didn't know what to do about it.

Much later I came to know that the term he was using did mean little Lara, but it was used as a term of love and endearment. It was a term a father would use for his daughter. Wow, that was a surprise to me!! I had the totally wrong perception of the name.

Think about this? I have heard it said that advertisers have concluded that the most attention-grabbing word that viewers react to is their name. I like it when in movies, someone calls out an actor's real name and the actor responds to hearing their name. And scripture in Psalms 147:4, tells us that God numbers the stars and calls them each by name.

Using someone's name in a conversation is very powerful. And I think there is power in the use of nicknames as well. I believe that God has nicknames for us. He calls us His child, He calls us His masterpiece and He calls us be-lov-ed!

Isn't it wonderful that God chooses to call us His child and not only that we are his children, but He calls us be-lov-ed! I am loved! You are loved! We are loved!

When we were on the mission field, in our newsletters and communications back in the States, we chose to refer to praying to God as "Talking to Daddy." It helped with any problems that could arise by asking for prayer, but it also gave me the picture of a little child crawling up on her daddy's lap and talking to her daddy. I believe this is a perfect picture of who God is; our Father, our Daddy!

Chapter Two
Growing Up with Hard Work and Play

    From Spring through Fall, we planted the garden and weeded the garden (truck patch) and brought in the goods at harvest time. Sometimes it felt as if that was all we did. Remember, we were feeding a family of 12. But Daddy was great at treating us well. Some summer nights after a long day of weeding the garden, he would take us to New Holland Twin Kiss (local ice cream place) and treat us to ice cream cones. My favorite was a vanilla and chocolate twist soft-serve cone. Or sometimes he would buy a large watermelon and treat us to that.
    At harvest time, there was always plenty of work to be done. There was endless cleaning and snapping beans. There were always between 8-10 half bushel baskets full. We would put newspapers on our large dining room table and dump the beans out for all of us to clean and snap. We would do the same for hulling peas. We would all sit around the table and do the work together. Mom would get us up very early when it was time to pick the corn. She would pick it and we would carry it from the garden to the yard. We would put out our hands and arms in front of us and she would pile the corn on our arms with as many as we could carry. We would take them to the yard and put them in a huge pile. Then we began the long hours of husking the corn. Mom would pick the tomatoes and put them in half bushel and full bushel baskets, and we would carry the baskets to the yard. We could carry the half bushel baskets up to the house, but when daddy bought a little tractor with a trailer, we would haul the baskets up to the house using the tractor. We would pick cherries, strawberries and raspberries. We also had to pick concord grapes, pears, apples, white and purple plums. They were in much smaller amounts and didn't yield as many baskets. Daddy would use a digger to dig up the potato plants, and sweet potato plants, and we would walk through the rows, most of the time barefooted, and pick up the potatoes and sweet potatoes. Mom would often dig up the carrots and picked the cucumbers and squash. They didn't yield as many baskets, but they all had to get carried or moved up to the house. Then there was always mowing to be done.
    After the vegetables were clean and the fruits washed, mom would prepare the fruits and vegetables for freezing or canning. Most of the vegetables we froze for the winter. For tomato juice and

applesauce, we would use a cone sieve on a tri-pod stand with a wooden pestle. Bad stuff stayed in the sieve and the good stuff was pressed through the sieve. We made the applesauce and canned it, cooked the tomatoes for the tomato juice and canned it, we made apple butter and canned it, and made jams and jellies and canned them.

In the fall, we even took apples and pears to a local cider mill and had them make cider. We would get home from school and daddy would come home from work and announce that we were making cider tonight. We quickly got dressed (sometimes it was very chilly) and picked up apples until we had enough to fill the back of our station wagon so we could take them to the cider mill. We would take large milk cans along to the cider mill for the cider and then when we got home, we needed to dump the cider from the milk cans into gallon jugs. Within the next few days, we would take our wagon through the neighborhood to sell the cider by the gallon to our neighbors.

When it was time to mow every week, there were apples to be picked up (we had to be careful when picking up apples because the bees loved the rotten apples that were on the ground), black walnuts to be picked up, paw-paws to be picked up, and chestnuts (with the very prickly-pointed shells, so we would have to wear daddy's leather gloves) to be picked up.

One year daddy made a path the whole way around the garden for us to ride our bikes. Then, as the older children were moving out and there were fewer of us at home, we didn't need the entire garden, so daddy took a part at the end of the garden and made a large figure-8 for us to ride our bikes.

One summer, some friends from church got tired of us saying we had work to do in the garden when they wanted to do something fun together. Sometimes it felt like we had unending work to get the produce out of the garden. They didn't have a garden and didn't know what we were talking about, so they came for a day to help us and see what it was like to take care of a garden.

Being from a large family and both mom and dad were from large families, when we had Reunions, there were always lots of aunts and uncles and lots of cousins. Maybe once or twice a summer, we took day trips to Elk Neck State Park in Maryland and French Creek State Park in Pennsylvania to go swimming with 2 of mom's sisters and their families. For a few years, daddy would take 1 day out of his vacation time, and we made a day trip to Ocean City, New Jersey or to Ocean City, Maryland.

    Daddy's mother started a family gathering when I was just a baby on Thanksgiving. Every year we got together on Thanksgiving Day at Noon for our Thanksgiving Dinner. Everyone would bring something to share for this meal. One year daddy and his brothers (or their wives) would make the turkey and gravy and then the next year it would be the girls turn to make the turkey and gravy. Mom and dad and his brothers and sisters and their spouses would get together for a meal to discuss what else was needed to complete our Thanksgiving meal. They would each have an idea of how many from their individual families would be in attendance so they could plan the amount of food needed. Then that information was given to the children and grandchildren. They would tell us that they needed 2 or 3 quarts of peas, 1 quart of fruit cocktail, or 4 pumpkin pies, etc. We would all choose what we wanted to bring. This family Thanksgiving gathering started at the family farm on Peters Road in Leola. When I was in elementary school, we moved to gathering at the old building of Bareville Firehall (Leola) until the mid-nineties, which has been torn down. For many years we used China plates and real stainless silverware. After the meal, the kids would play outside or inside depending on the weather and the grownup ladies would wash the dishes. They had a dumb waiter in the firehall to move the dishes from the main dining room to the basement where they were stored. I remember being fascinated as a little kid to learn how the dumb waiter worked. We would run upstairs to see the ladies load the dumb waiter with the dishes and then when they would send the dumb waiter downstairs, we would run downstairs to see it come down and watch them take off the dishes. Soon the family outgrew the firehall, we numbered over 150 people gathering for Thanksgiving. As I was one of the younger children of my family and my dad was one of the younger children of his family, most of my cousins were a lot older than me. Most of my cousin's kids were my age. Eventually we ended up meeting in the fellowship hall of the family's home church, Groffdale Mennonite Church, for many years. In 2014 we stopped meeting as the large Martin Family for Thanksgiving, because a couple of my cousins didn't want to do such a large gathering and wanted to have Thanksgiving with their own families in their own homes. It was a very sad time. We have had a few summer or fall gatherings for the cousins and the girl cousins have gotten together several times too. But the only other time we see each other now is at funerals. My mother said that we would continue to get together for her family on Thanksgiving and we have done that for over 10 years. Since there are 10 of us children, we take turns, of course, in age order, planning our meal and everyone brings something to share in our meal.

The big old white house where I grew up in Bareville had 5 bedrooms. Bareville used to have its own post office, but when they got rid of that we used Leola's post office and zip code. The biggest bedroom was in the back of the house. Daddy built a double bed bunkbed for the youngest 6 girls for that room. We slept 3 in a bed until the older girls got married or moved out.

Thinking about growing up in that old white house brings back many memories. One memory is of jumping off the balcony at the back of the house. Mom and dad were quite upset that we were jumping from the second story. At the time, we didn't see anything wrong with it and we had a lot of fun. Until I got a little older, the distance to the ground from that balcony somehow grew and it wasn't fun anymore to jump that distance. Other memories are of lying out in the sun, washing our cars in the backyard over the summer, and using the water hose to cool ourselves off in the summer. Daddy and the boys as I remember always had motorcycles around that they rode. I don't think any of the girls rode them. One time, Daddy bought a minibike and mostly the girls rode that bike. One time, I decided I wanted to ride that minibike on the garden path around the garden. I got to the first turn and my hand actually went down, and I revved the engine instead of turning the handlebar. With the revved engine, I sped straight into the raspberry bushes and the fence at the edge of the garden. Well, that really shook me up. I picked up the minibike and stood up. I wasn't hurt real badly and the minibike was just slightly bent. I couldn't believe I just wrecked the minibike. I think I was more upset with myself than actually hurt, and I walked up to the house, crying the whole way. When I got to where daddy was working, I thought he would be very angry, but he wasn't. He only asked me if I was okay.

Some summers, we would get a vacation from the garden when we would have the opportunity to stay with Uncle Tom and Aunt Lucille for a week or two. They lived in State Line, Pennsylvania, which is now a 2-hour drive away. When I was younger, before some of the new highways were built, it was more like a 3- or 4-hour drive. And that was back when speed limits were more like 40 and 45 not the 65 and 70 of today.

My mom and dad lived in the State Line area shortly after they got married. My mom's oldest brother lived close by in Greencastle, and he told my dad that there was work there, so they moved. Shortly after they moved, they met Tom & Lucille Christophel. Tom and Lucille invited my mom and dad to their church and quickly they became just the absolute best friends. My mom and Aunt Lucille had black hair (for a few years they both dyed their hair black). Often mom and Aunt Lucille would dress in very similar clothes or colors of clothes. Even when mom turned 90, we had a large birthday party for her. Aunt Lucille was not able to attend, but about a month later, Aunt Lucille visited mom and they both were wearing the same color blouses. Daddy sang with Uncle Tom in a men's group at that church with 4 or 5 other guys. When we visited and attended church on Sunday morning, this group of guys would always be asked to sing in the Worship Service.

Some summers, we would have "Grammy" come and stay with us for a couple of weeks just at the time we were hulling peas. She loved to help, and we loved having her with us. Grammy had very long hair which she would wear in a bun. When Grammy would let her hair down, we often would brush it for her. We loved doing that.

Uncle Tom, Aunt Lucille (and Lucille's mother, Grammy) were not blood relatives, and they had no children of their own, but they treated us as if we were their own children. We got to do things we didn't always have a chance to do at home. We would be able to walk down the street to a little shop to buy candy. Aunt Lucille had a soda machine in her "Beauty Shop." Uncle Tom would always open it up so we could get a bottle of "pop." We got to ride bike on their back street which had little or no traffic (we grew up and lived along the very busy road of Route 23 in Leola). They had the "Highlights" magazine which was full of fun things for kids to do. Sometimes, they would just send the magazines home with us to work on them. We would sit on Aunt Lucille's chairs in the beauty shop and spin until our hearts were content. And we would always look forward to getting our hair washed and cut by her. Sometimes, she would come to Leola just to cut our hair and visit for a while.

If we were at their house on a Sunday after church, most of the time we would have at least another 10 or 20 people, some family and some friends from church, for Sunday lunch. After lunch we would get the food put away, the dishes cleaned, and then Aunt Lucille would start getting out the "fixins" for supper so we could get to Sunday night church on time. When we stayed overnight at their house, I remember hearing Uncle Tom & Aunt Lucille pray at night. That was always a very special time as they ended their day talking to the Lord.

When Uncle Tom and Aunt Lucille were building their new home, me and my other 2 youngest sisters got to go to their house over that summer and help them. We got to hammer the floorboards down in the rather large dining room/living room area. We were so proud to be able to say we helped to build their new house even though the boards were covered with carpet, and no one could see what we had done.

Singing as a Family. We sang at church. We sang at family reunions, when we gathered at relatives' homes, and we sang for Mother & Daughter Banquets at our church. One year, mom made dresses for each of the girls and even liquid embroidered roses (a kind of painting) on all of the dresses for us to wear when we sang at one of EUM's Mother & Daughter Banquets. I was the youngest at the time and I was probably about a year old. Over the years, we were able to keep only one of those dresses. My daughter even had an opportunity to wear that dress. A few years ago, one of my sisters took the only dress we still had and put it in a keepsake frame along with the picture that we had. So sorry, the youngest was not born yet. So, there were only 7 girls out of the 8 girls in my family in the picture.

Some of the songs we would sing were "The Upper Window;" "Trust and Obey;" "Christ the Solid Rock;" "The Old Rugged Cross;" "Amazing Grace;" and "Love Lifted Me."

Daddy loved to play his harmonica and was really good at it. It's amazing to me that he taught himself to play. His story goes like this: "I would sneak into my mother's room and grab her harmonica and go somewhere to play it. That's how I learned to play harmonica." I found it even more fascinating that my grandmother also played harmonica.

One special thing that daddy always did was to call us on our birthday to wish us a Happy Birthday. If we answered the phone, he would play "Happy Birthday" for us. If we didn't answer the phone and we had an answering machine; he would always play "Happy Birthday" for us.

After I learned to play guitar, daddy would play his harmonica, and I would play my guitar. We would play and sing together at most family gatherings. Our favorite songs were: "I'll Fly Away;" "Mansion Over the Hilltop;" "I Saw the Light;" "Amazing Grace;" and "The Old Rugged Cross." After I learned some songs in the Russian and Kazakh languages, as we sang, I would start singing in Russian or Kazakh. It would always surprise daddy. Some of those songs were: "This is the Day;" "Rejoice in the Lord Always;" "Praise Him in the Morning;" and "King of Kings and Lord of Lords."

We did have a piano in the house when I was growing up. My oldest sister took piano lessons. I wonder why none of the rest of us took piano lessons too. But I do know that we did try to play it. After I started to learn to read music in school because of singing, learning the trumpet and when I learned chords on the guitar, I figured out that I could play a chord on the piano and play the notes of the song and it would sound pretty good.

All through school from 4th grade up, I played the trumpet. I played in the concert band, and in high school we also had the marching band that I played in. I don't think my siblings liked it when I played my trumpet at home. Often, I would go outside in the farmer's corn field next to our house and hide in the corn and play my trumpet there. I did love playing the trumpet and I so loved all the other musicians in the marching and concert band.

Our marching band participated in a few competitions. I believe we took first place one year. We also marched in a couple of expeditions (no judging). They were a little less stressful. We marched in the New Holland Farmer's Fair Parade and the Ephrata Parade every year except when it rained. We also marched at our home football games. Our marching band uniform consisted of pants, a jacket, with a leather overlay, we wore leather spats (which were snapped around the ankle and covered the shoe), and a large hat that was about 12 inches high. Sometimes it was very cold, for the football games, I would stuff my coat in my hat and then I could wear my coat over my uniform while sitting in the stands to watch the game.

I joined the High School Chorus in my sophomore year. I loved singing with the group and challenging myself to learn the songs. When it came time to try out for "County Chorus," I worked at learning the extra music so I could try out. I made it all 3 years.

In my junior year of high school, having been accepted into "County Chorus" gave me the opportunity to try out for the choir called "American Music Abroad," a group that was going to travel to Europe over the summer. I was thrilled at the opportunity, but I think that my parents were even more thrilled, at least from my perspective as a 17-year-old. Since our ancestors were from Switzerland and Germany, I believe my parents always had a secret desire to be able to travel to Europe and they went above and beyond to make this trip available to me. They decided they would go to the bank and borrow the money I needed. Somehow, they did this just so that I was able to take this trip. What a sacrifice they made for me. I never heard anything more about it from them. However, when I got a full-time job after High School, I paid them back as I was able.

It was a very exciting trip; traveling with 200+ singers, orchestra players, band players, a small jazz band and we even had a color guard that travelled all together in several buses in Europe over a two-week period. The group consisted of high school students and college-age students from Lancaster County.

It was my first experience on an airplane, and I didn't do very well. Even though I took some motion sickness pills, I got sick on my way over. I have learned a lot since then about motion sickness, but I was only 17 then.

We traveled and sang in Italy, Germany, Netherlands, Austria, Switzerland, and United Kingdom (London). What a beautiful trip that was!

Chapter Three
Growing Up in the Church and Believing in Jesus

Mom and daddy took me to church, I believe, before I was even one week old. The church was a very big part of our lives. We had Sunday School and Worship on Sundays, Sunday night services, and Wednesday night fellowship. Both mom and daddy taught Sunday School for many years and daddy was always doing some kind of work around the church.

At a very early age, we would sing in the Choir, we would be a part of Children's Day Services and had to learn recitations and then say them in front of the congregation. The 2's and 3-year-old classes would sing, the 4-year-old class would sing, and the kindergarten class would learn recitations and sing. We had Primary Department (1st grade through 3rd grade) Sunday School and Choir and classes on Wednesday nights. The Junior Department (4th grade through 6th grade) Sunday school and Junior Choir and classes on Wednesday nights. The Youth (7th grade through 12th grade) had Sunday school classes, a Youth Choir and we had Wednesday night and Sunday night Youth Group. After high school graduation, we would move to the Adult Choir.

I loved growing up at EUM Church in New Holland. We lived in Leola, so we went to Conestoga Valley School District, but almost all my friends at church lived in New Holland so they went to Eastern Lancaster County School District (Garden Spot School). However, I did have a few friends at church that went to Conestoga Valley School. I loved all the activities we had as children, Sunday School, Worship Service, Choir, Summer VBS, Missions Weekends, Youth Activities, and Christmas Eve Services.

Having been in the church from an early age, I was about 11 years old when I publicly accepted Jesus as my Lord and Savior. I memorized scripture and recalled them many times in my life. These are a few of my favorites that I remember saying often throughout my school years to keep me focused on Jesus and his love and work in my life:

Seek ye first the Kingdom of God and His Righteousness and all these things shall be added unto you.   Matthew 6:33

Trust in the Lord with all your heart and lean not unto your own understanding in all your ways acknowledge Him and He will direct your path. Proverbs 3: 5 & 6

Delight yourself in the Lord and He will give you the desires of your heart. Psalm 37:4

In high school, we had a 9-week music course which was guitar lessons. One of my sisters, who is 2 years older than me, had that course, so my parents bought her a guitar for her 16th birthday. I think I may have picked up her guitar and played it more than she ever had it in her hands. So, by the time I got to that high school class, I already knew a lot. For my 16th birthday, my parents gave me a guitar.

As a youth/young adult, I helped a lot with the children's ministry at EUM. I remember leading many Sunday morning children's Sunday school opening time with my guitar and singing. I also led the children to sing for Vacation Bible School. When missionaries would come to EUM to tell us about their work, they would teach me some songs in their language so I could teach them to the children.

One of the very first songs I learned on the guitar was "They'll Know We Are Christians by Our Love" and I quickly taught that song to the children. We sang "Pass It On;" "I Have Decided to Follow Jesus;" "God is So Good;" and many others.

As soon as I learned how to play the guitar, I jumped right in to play for our youth group meetings at EUM every week and at retreats. We would always sing at least a handful of songs. For a time, the youth group even traveled every Sunday night to a nursing home. We would begin with singing songs and then our youth leader would give a message. Many of the songs were scripture verses put to music. What a great way to memorize scripture. We even sang on Sunday mornings when the youth were allowed to sing in Worship.

The following is a list of some of the songs from scripture texts that we sang, all from the King James Version:

Beloved Let Us Love One Another - I John 4:7 & 8
Make a Joyful Noise Unto the Lord - Psalm 100
The Lord is My Shepherd - Psalm 23
Behold What Manner of Love the Father has Given Unto Us - 1 John 3:1

Trust in The Lord With All Your Heart - Proverbs 3:5-6
Therefore the Redeemed of the Lord - Isaiah 51:11
Rejoice in the Lord Always - Philippians 4:4
Rejoice Always, Pray Constantly, Give Thanks in All Circumstances - I Thessalonians 5:16, 17, 18
This is My Commandment - John 15:11-12
I Will Sing Unto the Lord for He Has Triumphed Gloriously - Exodus 15:1-2
Ho Everyone that Thirsteth - Isaiah 55:1
They That Wait Upon the Lord - Isaiah 40:31
Create in Me A Clean Heart - Psalm 51:10-12
Clap Your Hands All You People - Psalm 47:1
Great is The Lord - Psalm 48:1-2
Seek Ye First - Matthew 6:33

One year, our church had a Passover Seder to teach the folks about the meaning behind the Jewish Passover Seder. The folks that were leading the service, asked me to learn the songs in Hebrew so that I could lead and teach the congregation.

I was not a part of Youth for Christ (YFC) in our area while I was in High School. However, after High School I started going to YFC Alumni Group (for college and career age). I joined with the other guitarist to help lead all the singing time for our YFC group on Friday nights, including when we went to Ocean City, New Jersey for a week every summer.

Chapter Four
Meeting David and Our Lives Together and
Ministry With David and Adoration Ministries

Shortly after I graduated from high school, I started my first job working at New Holland Farmers National Bank. I worked in the credit department and had a very good job there until I changed jobs after I was married. Then by the fall, mom and dad sold our home in Bareville (Leola) and moved into a home in New Holland. My one brother and my younger sister were living with us at the time. Soon my brother moved out and got married and my sister got married and moved out. So, it was just mom, dad and me for a few years.

Music has always been a very important part of my life. After graduating from high school, I really missed singing in groups like chorus. I sang with my church in all the appropriate age choirs all through school. But after singing in school chorus and playing trumpet in the band for concert band and marching band all through school, I missed being a part of those larger groups creating music together.

During the summer of 1981, EUM had an outside group named Continental Singers come for a concert at our church. As they sang, I could feel all those wonderful emotions well up inside of me. The singers told us during the concert that they would hold open auditions after the concert for folks who wanted to be a part of Continental Singers. Of course, I went to the front of the church and auditioned! I don't even remember what I sang that night. I was so excited about the possibility and after auditioning and getting the "green light" to submit an audition tape to their organization, I went home on cloud nine! All I needed to do was put together an audition tape of 2 songs and send it to them.

In the next few weeks as I started to think about songs to put on that audition tape, I was made aware of a local Christian music group called "Adoration" that was looking for additional members. For some reason, unknown to me at that time, I was drawn to audition for "Adoration." It was an interesting audition; the leader only wanted a guitar player not a singer. However, after playing several songs, the leader asked me to sing along with playing my guitar. I was accepted and asked to come to a meeting as they were coming back together after having taken a break over the summer.

There were other individuals who were also invited to join Adoration and come to that same meeting.

That first night I met a guy who was joining the group at the same time. His name was David Potts. Later, after David and I were married, we would always talk about him growing up in Western Lancaster County and I grew up in Eastern Lancaster County and Adoration practiced mostly in Lancaster City, so we met in the middle - Lancaster City.

As Adoration practiced, I was asked to play several songs for David while he sang. I found out that David was also asked to sing solos at churches and events outside of "Adoration" and he began to ask me if I would play my guitar to accompany him. We did that several times and it was fun.

Adoration practiced together one night every week. After about 4 months, David asked me on a date. The only thing I knew was that we were going into Philadelphia to hear "The Messiah." This was in mid-December and his sister was going to be playing her violin with the Philadelphia Bible College Orchestra. David decided to make this date a double date with friends of his who were already married. We were so comfortable with each other; these friends didn't know this was our first date until David's pastor shared the story at our wedding.

We had a wonderful time stopping for supper on our way traveling from New Holland to Philadelphia. But as we got to "Broad Street," David pulled off the side of the road to park and commented that we just needed to walk a couple of blocks up Broad Street to the venue. Remember it was a December chilly night, and we were dressed in dressy clothes and dressy shoes… and 21 blocks later we arrived at our destination, just a little late. We had to wait until the end of the song they were playing for the ushers to open the door and direct us to our seats in the dark. We had to climb over others sitting in the row and I stepped on someone's toes as we climbed in; we were in and finally dropped to our seats. At the intermission time, the lights went on, everybody stood up and David proceeded to introduce me to his mom, his brother, many of his aunts and uncles, even his pastor and his wife. And guess what… the person who's toes I stepped on? You guessed it, it was David's mother's toes! She never held it against me. Honestly, I don't even remember ever talking about the fact that I stepped on her toes.

Shortly after that first date, David was asked to sing at a friend's wedding. So, he asked me to go with him. I remember sitting at the table at the reception across from a young boy who was 5 years old. For some reason, he decided he was going to talk with me. We had a wonderful conversation. At one point I asked him how old he was. His response was that he was 5. I said to him that being 5 was a wonderful age. And he said back to me that he thought it would be better if I would be 4 so he would be older than me.

One night David decided to take me to his mother's home in Mount Joy, Pennsylvania. We were traveling on Route 23 and drove through the small town of Silver Spring. The area looked very familiar. Suddenly, I recognized the road where my aunt and uncle had lived. When I said who my aunt and uncle were, David said, "Yes, I know your Uncle Leroy." It turns out that years earlier, David's father had carpooled with my uncle to their job at Hamilton Watch in Lancaster, Pennsylvania. Several times David's father had talked with David about knowing that Leroy had a brother who had eight girls, and David should get to know them. This was long after my uncle and aunt had died, and David's father had also died by this point.

It is a very interesting fact that David's father knew my uncle and it wasn't until many years later that David and I met. David also knew many of my friends with whom I graduated, and his sister was even at my high school graduation. Small world?

Adoration had several pianists, several guitarists, a bass guitar player, and a drummer. That first year or so, I believe we practiced more than we ever played out anywhere, except for a few churches of some of the members of Adoration.

One church we were asked to go to was on the southern end of Lancaster. I was given directions, but I had not previously driven in that area before, so it was confusing for me. Those two roads heading south from Willow Street, in my opinion, have several names. I was told to go down Route 222 from Willow Street. But I got confused and went down 272 South. I drove quite a while, and I could not find the street where I was to turn right. I finally stopped at a little corner shop on my left and asked for directions. It turned out that I was on the wrong road heading south from Willow Street, but the little road at that corner store was the very road I needed. It just came in from the opposite direction. I have no doubt that God has always been leading me and guiding me and helping me to take steps in my journey.

In October of 1982, David and I went to a conference that was held at EUM. It was a beautiful evening, and we decided to walk. On our way home, we were having a wonderful conversation as we walked. We crossed this one street and as we stepped up on the sidewalk, we stopped. David turned to me and said, "I wasn't planning to do this tonight, but will you marry me?" I said, "Yes." We both looked up to realize that we were standing on Union Street and we both thought that was funny!

We walked and talked the rest of the way to my home and then sat on the porch for a while and talked. I can't remember why, but we decided that we would not tell my parents that night. We did decide to wait until the next night to tell them. When we told my mom and dad, they both said that they knew and were not surprised. David had not told them, they just knew. I told David that I really wanted a December wedding, but this was October and there was no way we could plan a wedding that quickly, so we decided on December 3, 1983, and set our date. That year was so much fun as we planned our wedding and talked about our future together.

Many times, the members of Adoration expressed a desire to go to Lancaster County Prison to sing our songs, but I was not quite on board with that. As I would drive through Lancaster City, I would always get on the outside lane driving around the prison on Orange Street or on King Street. It turned out that as we contacted the prison, the doors were not open to us. I was so relieved!

As we continued to practice and time went on, it started to feel as if the whole group of Adoration was falling apart, so a special meeting was planned. David and I decided that we would go to the meeting, and we would probably tell everyone that we were going to drop out. As the whole group gathered, one by one, member after member shared that they would be leaving Adoration for one reason or another. In the end it was going to be David, me, and the drummer, Carroll Hughes.

"Wow, where do we go from here?" we asked ourselves. Well Carroll bought himself a guitar and taught himself to play, so we began with two acoustic guitars and David, and I sang. We decided that we would do the songs we had been singing in our individual churches, mostly praise and worship music and we stood on the passage of scripture found in Psalm 40:3.

"He has put a new song in my mouth, a hymn of praise to our God, many will see and fear and put their trust in the Lord."

At this time, we decided to reach out to Lancaster County Prison again, and almost immediately the doors were open to us. We commented to ourselves that when we had a larger sound, a more contemporary sound and a full band, the doors of the prison were not open to us. However, now that we only had 2 guitars and 2 or 3 voices, as sometimes Carroll would sing, the doors were open. We also went from singing lots of different kinds of songs to singing praise and worship songs and old hymns of the church. Now, the doors were open to minister in Lancaster County Prison.

By the time we needed to sign the paperwork releasing the prison from any responsibility if we were harmed while we were inside the prison, I no longer felt it necessary to drive on the outside lane around the prison. It was a matter of prayer, and I had prayed until I could sign those papers.

At Lancaster County Prison, we were on an every 7-week Sunday schedule. We would do 3 one-hour services each time; two in the early afternoon and one after dinner. Entering the prison was a very interesting experience as we stood in the lobby with all the friends and family members waiting to visit with their person. Then we were guided through the gates toward the chapel. We would be ushered through one gate; the gate clanged loudly, and it was closed behind us before the gate in front of us would be opened. We would walk through several of these passages and double door areas to get to the far end of the prison where the chapel was located at that time.

Back then, the chapel at Lancaster County Prison was a small room kind of in the shape of a triangle. The small stage they had for us was opposite the only door to the room. The room was filled with chairs. We set up our sound system and instruments and then we normally waited for a few minutes. The guards ushered the inmates into the room to sit in the chairs and then the guards stood in the doorway. The guards were not even in the room.

I remember one particular service. There was a young man sitting near the front of the chairs. We had never seen him before this service. What we found kind of unnerving was that during the talking and singing, even when David asked the guys to close their eyes, this young man kept his eyes open and on David. We didn't know what was going on. David shared that he was having trouble concentrating on what he was sharing and the words of the songs we were singing because this guy would not close his eyes. David was sure this guy was thinking about doing something, but just what David didn't know. David kept thinking if this guy was going to do something, the guy was between him and the guards. Little help the guards would be if he decided to do something. However, David continued to sing and speak, and we continued to sing the songs we had planned. As soon as we finished this service, this guy was the first one up to talk with us. He was crying and making gestures, not really talking. This young man kept pointing to heaven and gesturing that he saw Jesus when we were singing. So, we assumed that the Lord was ministering to him, and we didn't have to know what was going on.

After the chapel was empty, the chaplain asked us about this guy. He asked us if we had seen this young man before this Sunday. We said that we did not. The chaplain explained that this young man was deaf and mute. So, indeed, God was ministering to him in the way that this guy needed. God always communicates and even went beyond what we were saying or singing to connect to this young man.

Another time, as David was sharing, he asked the inmates, (without thinking of what he was saying) "Do you know what it means when we put up our hands in the air as we sing our songs?" As soon as the words came out of his mouth, David said to himself, "Oh no, what did I just say? Of course, they know what it means to put up their hands in the air. It is an act of surrender." David said to the guys, "Of course you know because you would have had to lift up your hands in surrender to the officers." To us, lifting up our hands as we sing our praise songs, we are surrendering to Jesus."

Many times, we watched the guys in the prisons come into the chapel with eyes downcast. After they listened to the songs of faith, after they were in worship, they were changed just because the Lord met them in worship. They left the chapel with their heads held high and a whistle on their lips, usually one of the songs we had sung.

We began a monthly prayer and Bible study calendar that we would send to the inmates. We then contacted other State Prisons in Pennsylvania and soon we were on a schedule of ministering 2 or 3 times a year in several state facilities, Muncy (Women's Prison), Camp Hill, Frackville, Dallas, Allenwood Federal Prison, and PICC (Philadelphia Industrial Correctional Center), which was super maximum security. I just recently learned they now have women in this super maximum facility. We would share our music; David would usually give a brief message and sometimes Carroll or I would share a thought about what God was teaching us or what a particular song meant to us.

As we continued to travel and minister in these prisons, we sensed God leading us to start a pen-pal program to connect church people with the inmates that wanted a pen-pal. However, that didn't last too long, because the church people would not follow our rules of the program, so we had to shut that down. We did, however, continue to send out our prayer and Bible study calendar monthly to about 200 inmates.

As we were traveling quite a bit, we decided to purchase a used van to make it easier to travel with all of our instruments, our sound system and the 3 of us. We put many miles on that van. It was an old chevy van and at one point, it broke down on the highway in Lancaster and it needed some major work done. A friend recommended a garage run by a Christian man that could do the work on the van. It took a little while, but when we got the van back it seemed to be running fine.

However, we were very aware that we needed to drive the van quite a bit that week as the weekend was approaching, and we had scheduled a major trip for a concert in a church in northern Pennsylvania. Everything seemed fine until part way to our destination, we thought something might be going wrong with the van. When we pulled into the church parking lot, we didn't just think something was wrong, we knew something was wrong. Carroll had been driving, and he said it felt like the engine had seized up. We called some friends from this church, and they located a car mechanic who was a church member to check it out for us. This mechanic took care of the van because we needed to get unloaded and set up in the church for that concert/ministry that night. When we finished for the evening, we were told that the engine was shot, that we had lost all our oil and that we could not drive the van. We were looking at a 4-hour drive home and had all the instruments and equipment to deal with.

The mechanic that checked out the van recommended that we take it to their local vo-tech school to install a new engine as they would do it free of charge because they were learning how to be mechanics, if we purchased another engine. This mechanic would work out all those details. Another friend in this church let us borrow a car so we could get home. We loaded the car with all that would fit in the car, and we headed home. We had to wait for at least 3 weeks until we could make the switch with the vehicles.

We knew that clearly the work that was done on the van in Lancaster before the trip to northern Pennsylvania was faulty. So, we had to discuss the situation with the mechanic that did the work here in Lancaster County. When David explained the situation to this man, he did not take ownership for the faulty work. We wanted him to at least take some responsibility and agree to pay for half of the price of the new engine. He would not.

So, guess what happened next? That very next Sunday, all 3 of us (David, Carroll and I) heard our preachers speak a message about forgiveness. After those messages and much prayer, we knew that God was telling us to forgive this man. We were able to forgive him, but we felt we needed to write a letter to describe what God was telling us to do. David was very angry, so he felt it was important for him to write the letter so that God could work through his writing to help him deal with his anger. Finally, the letter was written, and we could send it to the mechanic. It was done. We did not hear anything back, but we knew we did what God wanted us to do.

During this time David and Carroll had written several songs; David wrote most of the lyrics and Carroll wrote the music. David soon began to use the keyboard which activated a drum machine and the keyboard (both of which Carroll programmed) and Carroll started playing electric guitar, and I played bass guitar. (David had a dream one night and saw me playing a bass guitar and that the guitar was white. This was not the first time David had a dream as we stepped out in faith). When we woke up the next morning, David announced to me that I would be playing bass guitar. When we went to buy a bass, the only guitar they had in our price range was a white one. Between Carroll and me, we learned many rifts on the bass, and I played bass for about 4 years.

Around this time, we decided we wanted to record some of the songs we had written. We worked with a young man in Maytown, Pennsylvania who had a basement studio. To get ready, we practiced two nights a week and went into the recording studio one night a week. We finally were able to get a recording of some of our songs. This was back in the timeframe when recordings were on cassette tape. What a busy time that was. David was going to college, and

Carroll and I were working full-time at our jobs. My job just happened to be about an hour away of where we lived. We practiced about an hour away in the opposite direction and the recording studio was located another 20 minutes or so away, so we ended up putting many miles on our vehicles. After these practices and recording sessions, David and I would get home about 11:00 PM and then get up the next morning for work and school, and then do it all again, sometimes the very next night.

During this time, we not only ministered in prisons, but several nursing homes too. We felt as if the people in prisons and those in nursing homes were in the same boat. The folks in the nursing homes were prisoners in their bodies and in their sicknesses. We enjoyed being with both the inmates in prisons as well as with those living in nursing homes.

At this time, there was an Alzheimer's Home in Lancaster, Pennsylvania where we were able to minister. We enjoyed singing some of our original songs as well as praise and worship songs, but it wasn't until we sang songs like "The Old Rugged Cross;" "Amazing Grace;" and "How Great Thou Art" that we noticed the people were singing along with us. They began to settle down; they were not as fidgety and were really paying attention. Some of the people sat up straight and actually looked at us and sang along as we sang these hymns of the church.

The next week we received a very kind letter from one of the social workers at the Alzheimer's Home. She asked us what we did when we were there, because the residents were having a very good week. They were not running around getting lost and trying to escape. They were getting along with the other residents better than they ever had. All we could say was that we were worshipping the Lord, and that music is God's way of speaking to us, helping us, and ministering to us. The social worker was very excited as she was looking into music therapy, and this was some proof to her of how music works as a form of therapy.

We were asked one summer to work with a team from The Worship Center (local church) who traveled to Baltimore and worked in some of the government high-rise buildings. They would travel to Baltimore and lead Bible studies and prayed for the people in some of the worst areas. One summer, the leaders decided they wanted to do some outreach work in the area where they worked. The leader asked us to travel with him and share our music ministry.

After we shared our music, the leader would preach and then they would hand out sandwiches. The leader was given permission to close a street and make an area where we could set up our musical instruments and sound system and a space where we could preach. Sometimes we were in a small garden area, sometimes we were in a parking lot or courtyard next to the government housing. Extra folks from the leader's church always traveled with us and prayed for us. They prayed for our protection and prayed for the people who would hear the Word of God.

One particular Saturday, we were singing our praise songs, when David turned and started to preach to the building which was behind us. David felt that people were not coming out to the courtyard because they didn't want to be seen, so they were standing on their porches or at their windows. The one thing we were sure of is that they could hear the words we were singing, and they could hear the words he was saying. Shortly after David started preaching to the building, we sensed the presence of the Holy Spirit. It was a very sunny day, but a cloud rolled in and enveloped us. That was an awesome experience. I felt as if I was being hugged and loved in a very special way.

As David was preaching, a young woman came running up to us. She said she was up in her apartment and ran down 10 flights of stairs because she sensed God was there and she wanted to be where God was. We knew it was the presence of the Holy Spirit, as in that moment there was a healing. A young child who was being pushed in a wheelchair, got up out of her wheelchair and walked for the first time in her life. It was definitely a God moment!

We had an opportunity to work with the Salvation Army in Chester, Pennsylvania, singing and praising the Lord and telling the folks that would listen who God is and that God loves them.

We also ministered at Wernersville State Hospital and several other mental health facilities. Those were a bit more challenging, and we will never know this side of heaven, how God used us in those facilities.

Chapter Five
The Writing of "Gave Me You – A Song for Lori"

    Our first apartment did not have a laundry, so early in our marriage, one evening when I came home from the laundromat, David said to me, "I need you to get out your guitar." I said, "Okay." He said, "I need you to get your guitar and play a G… a D… and an A…" I said. "OKAY!" I thought to myself. Where did he get those chords from? He doesn't know anything about playing chords and especially he doesn't know anything about playing those chords on the guitar. So, I got out my guitar and started playing those chords like he asked me to do. As I was playing those chords, he started singing some words. And a song was being written.

    David took that melody and the words he wrote to our friend, Carroll, in Adoration, who arranged the song and added some additional music to the three chords. And "Gave Me You: a Song for Lori" was written.

"Gave Me You:" a Song for Lori
by David W. Potts, Lyrics
and Carroll Hughes, Music
© *1984*

Gave me you to share my life
My whole life through.
Gave me you to care for
As my wife.

God in all His wisdom and grace,
Gave me you.
He has blessed me beyond my dreams,
And gave me you.

God in His great plan for my life,
Gave me you.
You were worth my waiting for.
He gave me you!

Gave me you to share my life
My whole life through.
Gave me you to care for
As my wife.

At that time, David and I would often be asked to sing at Valentine's Day gatherings or we would sing on a Sunday morning during Valentine's Day time. David would like to tell the people that by singing this song, that he would get out of taking me out to eat or something like that. That comment always received a big chuckle.

Chapter Six
Preparing for Full-Time Ministry

David is called to be a pastor. Shortly after we were married, David was awakened in the middle of the night from a dream the Lord gave him. David shared with me the next morning that the Lord told him to stop running and to prepare for full-time ministry for the Lord. David said there was only one thing that he asked of the Lord following this dream and that was that I would have to be as excited about this as he was. David shared later that he thought that I was even more excited. I was excited but also scared because I felt this was a big step and it was a scary step to take. I knew God was asking us to follow him where he was leading us, and this was a necessary step.

Prior to meeting David, he had sung solos in many churches and venues. He also sang with a local guys' quartet that traveled to different churches. David believed that to prepare for full-time ministry meant that he needed to go to college. But David had not even graduated from High School.

So, his first step was to get a GED. David bought one of those practice GED tests. He worked through the test once or twice and then took the test within about 2 weeks and he passed with "flying colors." He got in touch with Eastern College, (now Eastern University) and they accepted him for the fall term into the Sociology degree program. We knew that with David going to college, we would not only have to pay for college, but we were also losing his income, and we would have to rely on my income alone. As we made this decision, we knew that we would need to put off raising a family so I could continue to work full-time while David was in college.

David thought because of our work in the prisons that maybe God wanted him to become a chaplain in the armed services or in a prison somewhere. But he found out that to be accepted into a chaplaincy program, he would need to have pastoral experience.

David grew up at Stehman's Memorial United Methodist Church in Millersville, Pennsylvania and I grew up at Evangelical United Methodist Church (EUM) in New Holland, Pennsylvania. When we got married, we decided that we wanted to find a church that was our church. But that proved to be more difficult than we ever thought.

We attended several different churches but never felt like we were meant to be there.

One evening we ran into a pastoral friend. Actually, we arrived at this restaurant and the parking lot was packed. So, David went up to the door to look in. He discovered that it was packed inside as well, so he turned to walk back to the car where I was waiting. However, a pastoral friend was eating inside. He saw David and came running out to the parking lot to talk with him. David told him about what the Lord was showing him and the call he believed God had on his life. The pastoral friend mentioned that we could always attend his church in Gap, Pennsylvania, and so we did.

We had been attending for about a year when the church had a special meeting called a "charge conference." The church submitted David's name as a candidate for David to pursue ordained ministry. That was a Wednesday evening, and the following morning David received a phone call from the District Superintendent who said, "I have this church that needs a pastor, do you want to serve Price Street United Methodist Church in Chester, Pennsylvania?

We continued to live in our home in Gap and traveled to Chester on Sundays for Worship. It was a very small church, and the work was done by a very small group of people. David and I would sing in Worship, and I began leading the children in Sunday School. We discovered that most of the children that came to Sunday school were from the neighborhood and not from the congregation itself. When we began at Price Street UMC, there were about 15 people in attendance for Worship. After a while, we saw about 35-40 in attendance.

One Sunday morning when we arrived for Worship, one man arrived just after us (he was chair of the church council, chair of the trustees, and head usher). He looked at the bulletin and asked David about how one of the announcements was listed in the bulletin. He didn't like how David worded the announcement and then exploded and walked right up to David. He was very angry about this announcement and threatened to put David through the window. I don't think that the man was strong enough to do that (maybe in his younger years he could have) but he was a very large man and the threat was made.

The man walked out the front door and David immediately called his District Superintendent. There had been a couple of other church members in the room as this happened. But soon others arrived, and

David began the service. We even had Holy Communion that Sunday morning. I didn't sing or play my guitar because I was too upset. I cried through most of the service. I couldn't believe that this could happen in the church and that it happened about 20 minutes before the service was to begin. But David preached and even served Holy Communion. At the end of the service, David needed to explain what happened to the Chair of Staff-Parish Relations Committee because she arrived after the start of the service. The man who had threatened David had walked outside and proceeded to talk to the other folks as they arrived. We didn't know what he said to them, and we didn't want to know. We left that Sunday, and I never returned. A few weeks later, David was told by his District Superintendent that he needed to go back one more Sunday and preach, which he did. We felt badly for the rest of the church, as they had been growing, but the threat was made, and we honored the District Superintendent's authority in not returning as Pastor.

The fact that we were seeing about 35-40 in attendance at Worship is what we believe was behind the anger of this man. He was losing his control over the people in the church. So, he was lashing out in any way that he could.

We then began a year of David not serving as pastor and we went back to our church in Gap to heal and discern what God wanted next from us. It was a great time to be back in the loving arms of the people there. Several pastoral friends after hearing the story were concerned that David might not pursue being a pastor. But for us, God confirmed in our hearts that being a pastor was the right direction.

Chapter Seven
Amanda Born Into Our Family

We were certain that David should pursue becoming a pastor that he attended local pastor's school and became a "licensed local pastor" in the United Methodist Church. As the next year approached, David was asked to be the pastor of Chatham United Methodist Church in Chatham, Pennsylvania. At Chatham Church, I joined a small women's singing group. I also taught Sunday School and David, and I would sing every so often.

One Sunday morning David just so happened to mention while preaching at Chatham Church that we wanted to have children. We had been trying for a couple of months. By this time, we had already been married for 10 years. We had made the very difficult decision to put off raising a family while David was in college. As I continued to work, David, due to some health issues, had started taking fewer and fewer college courses, and taking on more and more pastoral responsibilities, so College was taking a lot longer than either of us ever thought it would.

After that Worship Service, a young mother in the church approached us and said that if we wanted to have children, that she would be available to care for our child while we both worked.

At this time, my boss at Eastern Seminary was also praying for me to get pregnant. I shared with him in a couple of staff evaluation meetings (you know the part where they ask you what your plans and goals for your life are?). I would always say, my hope and my goal is to be a mother. At the end of my evaluation, we would always pray about it. One time my boss told me that if I were to get pregnant, it would be okay to bring my baby with me to the office, as long as I got my work done. With this information and knowing that this lady was willing to take care of my child, if we had one, we soon found out that I was pregnant with our first child. By this point in time, we had been trying to get pregnant for almost one year.

I had a great pregnancy with very little morning sickness. I had heard that it was important to have something in the stomach to keep from having morning sickness. So, most mornings I would wake up around 4:00 or 5:00 AM on my own. I would make myself some eggs and toast, eat my breakfast and climb back in bed to sleep until it was time to get up for work with the alarm. I did not really have any morning sickness to speak of. The only thing that was off for me was that the Seminary where I worked had a café and at lunchtime if I walked near the café, certain foods being cooked sometimes would turn my stomach. I was able to continue to work right up until the very end. Even though I would come home from work, make supper, and then crash on the sofa until it was time to go to bed. I would get back up in the morning and continue that process for the last few months of my pregnancy. During the last month, every morning when my co-workers arrived at the Seminary, they would ask me, "What are you doing here?" I would answer them, "The baby is not ready yet."

My baby's due date was September 1. The doctor said that if the baby goes 2 weeks late, they would induce the baby. So, she did go 2 weeks late and the Monday of the week it was decided to induce, I woke up for work and saw some spotting of blood. I quickly called my doctor. He didn't think it was anything to worry about but because we were so close to the date for inducement, he said come on into the hospital and we will get this birth started.

They did induce, but the process still took a long time. They kept putting me in rooms where there were much younger mothers. Remember, we had already been married 10 years by this time. These young mothers would come in and have their babies in just a few hours and then go home, while I was not even dilating yet. It took so long that they kept moving me from room to room and I was not able to get any sleep. Family members would come into our room to celebrate the birth of these young mothers and make a lot of noise and then they would leave. Sleep was just not happening for me. However, our baby knew exactly the right moment to make her entrance.

On Wednesday, September 14, 1994, I was finally dilated, and the contractions were strong. The doctor made the necessary preparations, and I was wheeled into the birthing room. I watched as the doctor was getting everything ready. I remember hearing him say, "What happened to the contractions?" Almost immediately a contraction came, and Amanda Rae Potts was born. It kind of caught the doctor off guard but fortunately he was able to catch her and hand her to me. She was a little jaundiced, so they rushed her away and put her in an incubator. I really needed some sleep. I had not gotten any sleep on Monday night or Tuesday night, and it wasn't until I asked for the epidural that I took a short nap. So, I slept through the first couple of feedings until the nurse decided it was about time I nursed my baby. So, the nurse woke me up to begin feeding Amanda.

She was a very healthy baby. I only had about 7 weeks of time to be off work with her. I put together my paid time leave and my vacation and then I knew that I needed to return to work. I did return on a part-time basis at first but soon discovered that I couldn't be a part-time mom and part-time worker at the same time, and we made the decision for me to return to work full-time.

After several weeks, the mother who told us she would take care of our baby while we both worked, said that she couldn't take care of Amanda anymore. She said her boys were now a little older and she had forgotten how much care was needed for a new-born baby. She didn't have as much freedom to do what she wanted with her boys and so we were looking for someone to care for Amanda. David did a lot of the care and even his brother, James, helped a little bit.

I was also able to take Amanda with me to work many days depending on my workload. She quickly became the "Seminary's Baby." My co-workers, the staff, the faculty, and the students loved her. As she began walking, she made herself the "official greeter" for the whole Administrative Hallway at the Seminary. The Seminary at that time was in an old hotel so there was a long hallway where all the administration offices were located. So, she would walk from office to office and give everybody her "hellos" and her very warm smile. My co-workers all looked out for her, and I had no fear of her being with them.

Chapter Eight
A Move to New London UM Church and
A Work Trip to Kazakhstan

    When Amanda was 9 months old the following July we moved to the United Methodist Church in New London, Pennsylvania where David was appointed as pastor. We moved into the parsonage right next to the church building. This is the only home that Amanda remembers. It was an old Victorian home with 2 living rooms with pocket doors separating them. All the wood was finished in a natural wood stain with a pretty light rose color carpet throughout. A special delight was that there were fully grown Chinese Cherry trees lining the front yard along with a couple of white and pink dogwood trees.

    The kitchen was large, and I enjoyed cooking in this kitchen. I also enjoyed living in this home. Amanda had her own area for playing and keeping her books and playthings organized.

    The church had 2 services on Sunday morning with Sunday School between the 2 services in a separate building. There was a wonderful Sunday School teacher for the little ones who welcomed Amanda even though she was younger than the rest of the students in her class. David started an adult Sunday school class and a youth night on Sunday nights.

    The first service was traditional in nature, but they had no one to play the organ or piano. I started playing my guitar, which by this time I had a 12-string guitar, for the hymns and led the singing in this service. The second service was a little more contemporary, but they had an organist and a choir. After the first couple of weeks, the church had a welcoming luncheon following the worship services.

    They had a separate building where the fellowship hall was located, so we all were in that building after the worship services for lunch. David and I always sang together in Worship. For some reason that day, I just left my guitar lying on the front bench of the sanctuary when we went to the luncheon. When we went home, we did not walk back through the church, but around the church to our home next to the sanctuary building. On Monday, I thought to myself, "Where is my guitar?" I figured I probably left it in the sanctuary so I would look for it on Tuesday night at choir practice. When I walked in the sanctuary for choir, it was not in the front of the church which is the last place I remembered having it. I then walked into the back area of the sanctuary, and it was not there either. When I went home, I asked David if he had seen my guitar over at the fellowship hall building where his office was located. He said that he had not seen it, so we believed it was stolen or destroyed. We had heard that several folks did not like the guitar being used in the church services and we suspected they might have gotten rid of the guitar. When the rest of the congregation heard of the theft, a group of older women went together and gave us money to purchase another 12-string guitar. After we purchased my guitar, we had a special service during the worship service to dedicate this guitar to the Lord's work.

As the months went on, we had heard that the organist had been in a car accident prior to us starting at New London Church. Later she began to experience some severe back pain and numbness in her arms. She began to not show up more and more and we were starting to head into the Easter season. Well, David told me that we needed an organist and choir director for Easter and announced to everyone that I would be their choir director. I used instrumental CDs, and I played guitar to accompany the choir.

During this time, David and I attended as many Billy Graham Schools of Evangelism classes as we could. We were trying to learn as much as we could about evangelism. We also got to see some incredible areas in our country and Canada. Some of the places we went to were Asheville, North Carolina to Billy Grahams' Training Center, St. Louis, Missouri, and Halifax, Nova Scotia. We also attended as many other conferences and seminars as possible so we could learn about missions and evangelism. In 1998, we attended a conference where we met Johanna Stahl. Johanna was sharing about her work with a mission agency that she worked with and led teams to do Vacation Bible Schools in Karaganda, Kazakhstan.

Well, that was the first time we heard of Karaganda, Kazakhstan. We became fascinated with this new country we just learned about. We grabbed maps to try to find out exactly where this country was located. It was difficult, as at that time, the only maps we could get our hands on were old maps and they still had the Russian spelling of countries, states and cities which had Karaganda and Kazakhstan begin with a "Q." Karaganda was spelled, "Qaraghandy." And Kazakhstan was spelled, "Qazaqstan." We were not looking for it to begin with a "Q," so it took us a while to find out exactly where this country was located.

We had some wonderful conversations with Johanna and decided we would invite her to come to New London Church to speak to our congregation about her work in Kazakhstan. Johanna spoke at the first service, then spoke with our children in Sunday school, and then she spoke at the second service. She shared about the children and their need for vitamins. She also told us about the children in orphanages and how those children didn't have anything that they could call their own. Johanna shared that she was looking for people to join a mission team to work in those orphanages and work in the school the missionaries started in Karaganda that summer. By the time she finished speaking, David and I knew we would be going on that trip. It was a work trip scheduled for a little over 2 weeks, so Amanda at 3 years old was not able to go. Amanda stayed home with family and had her own little vacation traveling from home to home and being cared for by my parents, my brothers and my sisters.

Kazakhstan is a former Soviet Republic and is located south of Russia and West of China. Out of the 100 ethnic groups living in Kazakhstan today, the largest are the Russians and the Kazakhs. Most people speak Russian although the official language is Kazakh. Kazakhstan is the 9th largest country in the world.

Stahlin and his regime considered Kazakhstan to be a wasteland because of the extreme temperatures and because the land is barren and desolate. The temperatures can get as high as 110 degrees Fahrenheit or as low as 40-50 below. Dissident Russians were not only sent to Siberia but to Kazakhstan. Kazakhstan is actually southern Siberia. After the fall of the Soviet Republic, everyone that had the means to get out of Kazakhstan, did leave. There remained mostly Kazakhs and Russians.

The Kazakhs had been nomads. They would live out on the steppe which is grassland that extends some 5,000 miles from Hungary in the west through Ukraine and Central Asia (Kazakhstan) to Manchuria in the east. They would live in tent-like structures called Yurts. As they would graze their sheep, they could take down their Yurt and move their home from place to place. The sheep with their handsome, curly fleeces are pretty much a life support system for the Central Asian peoples, providing milk and cheese, meat, and warm woolen clothing. They would eat lamb and horse meat. A meal that is considered the national dish of Kazakhstan is named in the Kazakh language "Beshbarmak," which literally means 5 finger food. This is a meal they would eat with their hands, no utensils. It is a meal that resembles Lancaster County boiled version chicken pot pie just not as much liquid. The dish is made of horse meat or mutton, diced potatoes, onion slices, and pasta (like chicken pot pie pieces). One would grab a pot pie piece in their hand and then scoop up some meat, a potato and onion and eat it with their five fingers. They also would make "Shashlik" which is meat cut up and placed on skewers like shish kabob cooked over a fire. Sometimes there were also onion slices to eat with the meat. This meat traditionally is lamb, but could also be pork, beef, or chicken. We also came to love "Plov" which is a rice pilaf with lamb, carrots, onions and spices traditionally cooked over a fire. Sometimes it is made with beef or chicken. We also loved their flatbread, "Lepeshka."

David asked the ladies of New London Church to make "pew dolls," cloth-like dolls that we could easily take with us to give to these children in the orphanages. We also went to our local pharmacy and purchased as many bottles of children's vitamins as they had on short notice to take with us and that we could carry.

We started making all the necessary arrangements to go on this work trip. I asked for my vacation time, David asked for time off, but was only allowed by the church to take his vacation time. We applied for the necessary paperwork, and we also needed to begin asking our friends, family and churches, etc. for financial support to help pay for this trip.

Up until the Sunday before, we only had enough money for one of us to go on the trip, even though we continued to say that we were both going on the trip and making plans and packing for the trip. We believed that both of us were going on that work trip. That Sunday after church, when we went back to our home, the phone rang, and it was someone from my church at EUM asking me how much we needed to go on this trip. I told them the amount needed, and I was told that EUM would cover the remainder that we needed.

We had to drive to Atlanta, Georgia to meet the rest of the team that was going on this work trip before flying out. The team was made up mostly of people from a church in Michigan (several members of that church were missionaries in Kazakhstan). One or two members were from Kentucky, from the hometown of then current missionaries in Kazakhstan and a few from Pennsylvania who were going after hearing Johanna speak about the needs in Karaganda.

We drove to Atlanta and met the team at the airport hotel. We needed to spend a couple of days getting to know the team and the mission agency had some teaching sessions for us. But the night before we were to fly out of Atlanta, I was told that my visa finally arrived. No one had told me that it was not there. But God was in that arrival of my visa in time for David and me to both go on the trip.

We arrived in Almaty, Kazakhstan in the early morning hours, and we were ushered onto a bus the missionary team had hired to get us from the capital city of Almaty to Karaganda about a day's drive. I, again, had trouble with motion sickness on the plane and arrived feeling sick to my stomach. Over the years the motion sickness seemed to be not as extreme except for one flight that had severe turbulence. I think everyone got sick on that flight, including some of the flight staff.

The bus had no air conditioning, and the roads were very twisted and bumpy, which did not help. The missionary team that was traveling with us bought some snacks for us. So, I think I just had soda and crackers for a while.

About halfway to Karaganda, we stopped at a "restaurant" for a bite to eat. It was just an outside table next to a home out in the middle of nowhere. We were on the Steppes of Asia, it was very dessert like, and we saw several camels just roaming the Steppe. At the restaurant, we were served a cold potato soup. There were several very tiny pieces of something in the soup and we were told to not ask any questions and just eat (I believe it was probably horse meat). The hardest thing was to eat cold potato soup, but in the end, it really was not that bad. I had never eaten any soup that was cold. In my book, soup is supposed to be hot. It was just a "mind thing" that makes you say no to something that is so different.

Lake Balkhash was near this restaurant which is why we stopped there. After we ate, we all walked down to the lake. Some changed clothes to go in the water and some just went in with their clothes on. It felt really good being in the water after traveling for so long. Our flight was 15 hours with a 5- or 6-hour layover in the middle. Then we had to go through customs, and we just spent over 8 hours riding in a bus with no air and the windows were not able to be opened.

Lake Balkhash is the 15th largest lake in the world. It is 22,000 sq. kilometers (26 miles) deep. It is one of the most scenic places in

Central Kazakhstan. Its unique feature is that the eastern part is saline, and the western part is freshwater. I believe this may be the only lake to have both fresh water and salt water in the world. Before we got back on the bus for the remainder of the trip the missionary team cut open a fresh watermelon for us to eat.

The kitchen staff of the school our missionaries started in Karaganda had prepared our evening meal for our arrival in the city (we were to be there around 7:00 PM). We finally arrived, a little late, around 9:00 or 10:00 PM and had our meal. We received our instructions and our living quarters for our time in Karaganda.

David and I, and one other teammate went to the field leader's apartment. This was a Saturday night. We woke up Sunday morning and the whole team gathered at the school for breakfast. After breakfast we received a sack lunch of a hot dog and an apple, and we were told that after church we would be on our own to get back to our living quarters. Then we headed out to go to church. Sometime during Sunday night, one of our house mates woke up sick. I got up to sit with her and help her and then ended up getting sick myself. A large amount of our whole team ended up getting sick.

I believe the sickness hung on the longest for me. I was running a fever, I was nauseous, and I had diarrhea. It was 100 degrees with no air conditioning. The rest of the team were very concerned about me, so they scoured the city looking for a fan. They found only one fan in the entire city and bought it for me. We did have a missionary doctor on the team, so he was checking on me too. I slept most of the time and had the fan running constantly. David would change out an ice pack every time I woke up to go to the bathroom to help to cool me down. I remember mostly praying every time I crawled back in bed and every time I woke up.

I believe my body was very run down and therefore it was very difficult to get better. I had a very busy couple of weeks at work prior to the trip. The two weeks before the trip, I directed the Vacation Bible School at New London Church while working full-time at Eastern Seminary, plus preparing for the trip. I also needed to prepare for Amanda's care in our absence. After our return I still had a lot of trouble with nausea and diarrhea. After a couple of weeks, I went to the doctor back home and they discovered I had a parasite which they were able to treat.

Being sick, I pretty much missed the whole first part of the week of the work we had planned to do. We were scheduled to work at the school to remove/replace floors and clean and paint shelving units.

When I finally felt good enough to join the team, I was put on the job of scraping off old glue on the back of the linoleum that was pulled out of the school. They needed to put that linoleum back in the school because they could not find any new linoleum in the city to purchase.

We had an opportunity to go to an orphanage and deliver the vitamins we brought with us and to give out the "pew dolls" our ladies from New London Church made. It was wonderful to hand these dolls to all the children as we explained that they were their very own dolls to keep and take with them wherever they went. One young boy took the doll from me and immediately put it to his lips and gave it a kiss. It was a God moment.

We also did a lot of singing. The last thing we did was to start a church that was to meet in the hospital close by. We walked the streets and invited the neighbors around the hospital to a special Sunday service at the hospital. Some of the team sat at the bus stop and worshipped the Lord and prayed for everyone that was receiving the invitation.

Finally, on Sunday morning, the time arrived for the Church Service, and we found the doors locked to the room where we were to meet. So, we set up chairs in the hallway and had church. We ended up taking all the children outside to the hospital steps for Sunday school after the service and a church was started there. It was a very joyous time.

It was hard to leave Karaganda, Kazakhstan, we made friends with so many people including our teammates. David and I both felt that we would be returning to Kazakhstan. We kind of figured we would take our vacation every year and go back to Kazakhstan. It was only after getting home that we both started talking about sensing that God was calling us to the possibility of moving to Kazakhstan and becoming full-time missionaries.

Chapter Nine
One Step(pe) at a Time Toward Kazakhstan

"A journey of a thousand miles begins with a single step" is a common saying that originated from a Chinese proverb. The quotation is from Chapter 64 of the Tao Te Ching ascribed to Laozi, although it is also erroneously ascribed to his contemporary Confucius. This saying teaches that even the longest and most difficult ventures have a starting point; something which begins with one first step.

Meaning of One Step(pe) at a Time.... David always had a way with words, and he had a wonderful sense of humor. He could write and put words together that sometimes would make me laugh and sometimes would make me cry. But when David found out that Kazakhstan was on the Steppes of Asia, he could not resist to use those words somehow. As we prayed, we believed that God was taking us closer and closer to Kazakhstan one step at a time. So, our ministry phrase and the words we used just about every time we spoke became One Step(pe) at a Time, thus, the title of this book. We even used these words for the title for our communication to churches and folks who supported us and those who prayed with and for us. Our prayer newsletter became titled One Step(pe) at a Time.

We applied to the mission agency, but I remember standing in my dining room and spinning around to see all I could see from that point in my home and asking God if I was to get rid of everything I had. I don't remember hearing an answer. However, I believed He was asking me to take just this one step to be willing to give away all that I had and to take this journey one step at a time.

David looked at a possible schedule of raising support and getting to Kazakhstan and determined that he needed to resign his appointment of pastor at New London Church right away, so we could raise our support and prepare to move to Kazakhstan. We needed to be free on Sundays to go to churches to raise our support. We needed to raise enough funds for 5 years in Kazakhstan; four years as missionaries and 1 year back in the States to raise support again for the next 4 years.

I remember David telling me about his meeting with his District Superintendent and telling her about our decision for him to step down as pastor of New London Church. She was very supportive of how God was leading us.

We still needed to do some of the necessary testing and training needed by our mission agency. We had not yet been approved as missionaries, but we were sure that God was calling us. And we knew that if He was calling us then He was going to make the way for us. However, there were personality trait tests, there were psych tests and several trainings, interviews, and such to go through before we were even approved to be missionaries through this agency.

Because David was appointed to New London Church, and he was resigning from his appointment, we also needed to move from living in their parsonage. We decided that I would continue to work at my job at Eastern Seminary, so we were looking for a new home somewhere in Chester or Delaware Counties. We put that information in our newsletter to our friends who were praying for us, and we received a phone call from a friend who said to us that we needed to meet Marcia.

Marcia Bickley owned a home in Delaware County, and she had space available to rent in her home. She was a missionary and served in various countries for several weeks or months at a time. We set up a date to meet at her home and boy were we surprised. We pulled into her driveway and saw a beautiful stone home with very large trees lining the driveway. We learned that there were about 40 acres on her property.

To our surprise there was a large in-ground swimming pool in the backyard and a pool house that was bigger than any apartment we had lived in. We learned that she boarded horses. The location was perfect, within a half hour of the Seminary where I worked. We felt it was an answer to our prayers. But Marcia was so welcoming. She treated us like family. We had full use of her property and had 3 rooms and 2 baths of private space for us on the second floor of her home. The girls who boarded their horses even took care of the pool. When Marcia went on her mission trips, we would take care of her home and her beautiful dog. Her dog was very well trained and a great companion to us while we lived there. We enjoyed Marcia's company when she returned home from her mission trips until she headed out for the next trip. Our prayer for a place to move was so quickly answered. God showed up and we now had a home to move into. And to top it off, we also had a swimming pool! We didn't even ask for a swimming pool, but God went way above and beyond what we were even asking for. Moving into this home forced us to get rid of a lot of our belongings and start to prepare for a move to Kazakhstan. We lived in Marcia's home for 2 years until we were ready to attend Russian Language School prior to our move to Kazakhstan.

It was during this time that I experienced problems with my appendix. I was at work and I had pretty much worked through my lunchtime, but I felt hungry. I went to the snack machines and grabbed some type of snack to eat because it was late in the day and I didn't want to eat too much before the end of my day and then supper. But after I ate that snack, I still didn't feel quite right. It was a pain that I had never felt before. I decided to leave work early and headed home. David knew I didn't feel very well, so he took care of Amanda and went to the local fast food for supper as I went to bed. During the night, it felt like the pain traveled from my abdomen around my back and then settled back on my right side abdomen. When we woke up I told David about how the pain had traveled and he was sure it was my appendix. I don't remember if we took Amanda to school that day or if we got someone to watch her, but we headed to the hospital. It took them a long time, most of the day, to determine that it was indeed my appendix. They were trying to rule out everything else that it could possibly have been. By the time they decided on the surgery to remove my appendix it was close to bursting. That would not have been good. Anyway, the surgery was over, and when I returned home, I was in a good amount of pain. I took the pain medicine, but it made me feel so out of it and worse, that I decided I would not take that strong of medicine again. But here is a glimpse of David's humor. He picked up our cat by all four legs, turned him up-side-down, and waved him over my body. He told Amanda that he was giving me a "cat scan." We all laughed and that was hard to do while in so much pain. It helped Amanda to have a little bit of humor, so she wasn't so scared about her mommy hurting. Also during the testing for the appendix, they discovered that my gallbladder was inflamed and that I would have to have something done with the gallbladder. I told the doctor that we were planning to move to Kazakhstan. He said that I would have increasing amounts of pain with my gallbladder and that I would definitely want to get it removed before moving. We prayed about it and God healed me. I never had any pain with my gallbladder.

Because David resigned his appointment at New London UMC, we were asked to return to the church in Gap to be their music leaders for the time as we prepared to be missionaries. We were more free to travel on Sundays than if David was still a pastor. It was about this time in 2000 that David graduated from Eastern College (now Eastern University) with a degree in Sociology.

In July 2001, I resigned as Assistant to the Vice President for Advancement after working for 15 years at Eastern College/Eastern Baptist Theological Seminary. In 1986, I began working at Eastern College as secretary to the Alumni Relations Director of Eastern College. I also was secretary to the Church Relations Director of both Eastern College and Eastern Seminary. In 1991, I moved to working only for Eastern Seminary as Administrative Assistant to the Vice President of Advancement. Over the years, I worked for five Vice Presidents and as I was working for the last one in 1999, I was promoted to Assistant to the Vice President of Advancement of Eastern Seminary for the last two years.

In August of 2001, we rented a U-Haul truck and made our way to Columbia, South Carolina to the Russian Language School at Columbia International University. We rented a small trailer to live in close to the Russian Language Program, sight, unseen.

Well, we really felt like we were learning how to make a cultural move when we moved to South Carolina. The trailer had 3 bedrooms. Amanda had her own room which was at one end of the trailer. At the other end was our bedroom and through our bedroom was a back entrance. Except this back entrance is where the clothes dryer and washing machine were located. The dryer opened into our bedroom, but we needed to go out the main door outside to the end of the trailer and step up into the back door to use the washing machine. After the wash was done, I threw the wet clothes in the basket on the top of the dryer, walked around back to the main door and back through the trailer to our bedroom to put our clothes in the dryer. The way to fix the freezer door that would not stay closed properly was to use a bungy cord which was attached to a cupboard door. The front porch was wooden and falling apart, and the back porch was also wooden, and it was not even able to be used.

On September 11, 2001, we were sitting in one of our language classes, when someone came to the door and took our professor out into the hall. When the professor came back in and told his wife what was going on, her face turned white. She explained what was happening and the class was over.

We walked outside to see all the college students walking to the auditorium to watch the news coverage of the Twin Towers in New York City. Everyone was calling family and friends and trying to find out as much information as possible and trying to make sure that their family and friends were okay.

While we were in Russian Language School, we met Anne who was an elderly woman who supported our mission agency. Anne would reach out to students in the Russian Language program inviting them for meals and fellowship. We shared the pew doll idea with Anne and she took our idea and designed her own pattern for making pew dolls.

At this time, we learned about a friend of Anne's who was very crafty. Anne invited us to see this friend's crafts and to spend a little time talking with her. This friend was very discouraged at being old, living by herself after losing her husband, and just unhappy with the world as it was at that time. When we told her about the Pew Doll Ministry, she saw a way that God could still use her in this world to make happiness for children around the world. And she decided to get busy making all kinds of crafts for children and children at heart.

Anne began to reach out to teach folks in other churches and anyone that wanted to know how she made these dolls. And a ministry was started around making these pew dolls. She also made dolls for some other missionaries to take with them to their part of the world where they were going. She would investigate the dress and styles of the peoples and make the dolls to resemble the nationals. Over the years she made over 2,000 dolls which went to over 50 countries. When she made her 1,000th doll, she gave it to me to thank me for this ministry that she had to be able to keep busy and reach children all over the world. I thank God for Anne who in her later years started a ministry that was and is far reaching. Who knows what little girl or boy has one of these dolls?

In October we had an opportunity as a class in the Russian Language Program to go to Charleston, South Carolina for a day to enjoy the area for some R & R. We had a wonderful time, but the next morning I awoke to find that David's toe was all bloody. Over the summer, he had a blister on the bottom of his big toe that we believed to be healed. I didn't even know where the closest hospital was located. I took Amanda to school that day without telling her because her daddy wanted her to be able to do well at school that day. When I got home, I had to find out where the hospital was and then I took David to the hospital. I told Amanda after school when I picked her up and then took her to the hospital to see her daddy. The blister on David's toe had healed over but had not healed inside. So, now it had gotten infected, and they were telling us that the toe needed to be amputated. They removed only part of the toe at first but then had to go back in and take the whole big toe.

David was not able to complete that school session. I attended some days as I was able before David got out of rehab. But after David got out of the hospital, completed his rehab, and came home, it was very difficult to get to classes. We had a great bunch of missionaries in training in our classes. They were such a big support to both of us. They wanted to do something for David and decided that he needed a good entryway to get into our trailer. So, they built a large wooden patio/porch so that it would be easier for David to enter our trailer while using crutches or if he needed to use a wheelchair. Many of our missionary friends dropped off meals for us and some even took care of our laundry.

I took Amanda to school and picked her up every day from school but couldn't get to language school and keep up with the studies. I became David's 24-hour nurse as they showed me how to take care of his open wound, keep it clean and redress it every morning and evening. I was very scared as I didn't have any nursing training, except for the last-minute lesson before he could leave the rehab hospital. His care became my primary ministry as well as helping Amanda deal with her schooling and homework.

During this time, there were many very well-meaning family and friends who told us that maybe God was saying to us to not go to Kazakhstan, but we felt even more certain that we were to go.

The Russian Language Program and the mission agency allowed us to take the class again in the spring semester. I did okay in the class, but it was very difficult for David to concentrate and to keep up with the studies. In the end, he could understand the language better than he could write or speak it.

While we were preparing for the mission field and raising our support, we spoke in over 200 churches. After the services, many folks would come and say to us that they thought we were very courageous. And that they would never be able to do what we were planning to do.

For us, we didn't feel courageous, but it was a matter of obedience. We prayed asking if we were doing the right thing... that we were leaving family, friends, and our church and planning to move to Kazakhstan, take our then, 8-year-old daughter... get rid of most of our belongings and move to another country... to move to a place where we only knew a little of the language. We didn't even know where we would be living. We prayed and we had our friends praying. And the more we prayed, the more we were certain that we were to move to Kazakhstan.

Chapter Ten
Living in Kazakhstan

    Our first year in Kazakhstan, we lived and worked in Almaty, Kazakhstan as a part of Teen Challenge Kazakhstan, a program for drug and alcohol rehabilitation. Almaty was the first capital of Kazakhstan. At that time, it was the largest city and is located in the southern and easternmost point of the country. At that time, it was the only city where international flights would fly in and out of.
    Teen Challenge Kazakhstan had a boys' home, a young women's home, a young men's home, a working farm for young men, and a refugee home. That first year we lived in the boys' home which was a home for delinquent boys or boys without homes or parents who were living in the streets. It was located on the outskirts of the city. There were 30 boys living in the boys' home. The home was a very large building which also had enough space for a large auditorium used by one of the churches that Teen Challenge started. It had a locked and gated entrance which was secured by the boys taking turns to be the security team. There was a single mother of a teenager as the director. They had a treasurer/business officer, a cook whose children were in the program, a bus driver, and two couples that led the studies and work at the home for the boys. Out of the very large building, we were given 2 rooms for our family.
    When we arrived in Kazakhstan at 5:00 AM, we were picked up by the boys' bus driver and "Volodya" because he was able to translate for us. When we walked in the building, we walked through a large entryway, down a set of marble steps, through a large room, down a very long, dark, and dingy hallway to our 2 rooms. There weren't even any doorknobs on those 2 doors, just open holes. There was a single army cot in the one room for Amanda and two single army cots pulled together in the second room for us. It was a long trip, and we all crashed into our beds. At 10:00 AM, the leader of Teen Challenge knocked on our doors, woke us up and said we needed to get up. He dropped off some bread and jam, told us we needed to eat and then he was going to take us to the outside market to get some food.
    After that first day, we began eating most of our meals with the boys, which were sometimes prepared by the boys along with the hired cook. Breakfast was sometimes, kasha (a kind of porridge), sometimes cream of wheat (which I found to be very good), or

sometimes a cream of macaroni which was sweetened so the boys would eat it (that tasted terrible to me).

When the boys were in school, we were on our own for lunch. For supper, we would eat soup. It was mostly a brothy soup with a few small pieces of meat and some small, diced vegetables. Sometimes we were given "Gretchka" which is buckwheat that I didn't like at all. When I walked in the building and smelled it being cooked, it would turn my stomach, so we would eat bread and jelly if we had some in our rooms for supper. The boys' home was the most underfunded group at Teen Challenge. If someone gave them a piece of meat, it could last almost a month as they would cut it up so small and always leave an amount in the freezer for the next day or days. We would always buy extra bread when we shopped at the "magazine" (small minute markets, Kazakhstan style) where we could get bread, eggs, water, and cookies, etc. at the edge of our property so the boys would always have at least some bread to eat.

One time someone gifted the boys' home with a quarter chicken (leg and thigh) for a Christmas meal. We had mashed potatoes with that chicken and that was extremely delicious after only eating soup for many months. There was also a special meal they cooked only a couple of times they called "Roulette." It kind of looked like a large Italian calzone. It was a large pasta type meal which had some meat, potatoes, and vegetables in it and was steamed. The young women's home would make what they called "Manti" which was a medium size pasta type meal (about the size of a roll) filled with meat and steamed. It often had pumpkin or squash along with lamb or ground beef. The women's home would sell their Manti as a fundraiser, and I would always try to buy some. It was very tasty. Sometimes we had "Pelmeni" which is a much smaller pasta (a little smaller than ravioli) filled with meat and boiled or fried. The best meal I think I remember is when they made Borscht (a cabbage, beet, and potato soup) served with a dollop of sour cream. I think some people eat borscht cold, but I was thankful that they made it hot. They would make it for Sunday night supper every so often and it was so delicious. It had a little more substance to it than the usual brothy soup.

After a while, we were able to take an adjacent room to our rooms and make it into a kitchen/dining area, and bathroom for our family. We made more meals for ourselves once we had the kitchen but still continued to eat with the boys as often as we could. Up to that point, we ate most meals with the boys. We were able to put a washing machine in our small bathroom, which made life easier.

    We also used the same bathrooms. The bathroom just so happened to be down that very long, dark and dingy hallway from our rooms and across that very large open room. There was one bathroom for the girls with 3 stalls (Kazakhstan style bathrooms are just holes in the floor). The girls' bathroom at least had doors on the stalls, however, they were only about 3 feet high. Amanda and I only had to share the bathroom with about 5 or 6 other ladies. Unfortunately, for David, he had to share the same bathroom with all the 30 boys who lived there. The boys' bathroom had 3 stalls (remember, Kazakhstan style bathrooms are just holes in the floor) but the boys' bathroom stalls had no doors. That would be very difficult for any man. Plus, the washing machine was located in the ladies' room, and we could not use it until the boys were finished washing their clothes. So, it was a real big deal when we were finally able to have our own bathroom and washing machine.

    Banya Experience. I had heard only a little bit about Banyas in Kazakhstan. I had heard that our director grew up going to Banyas and wanted to take us to experience the Banya. I really didn't know everything about it and when she invited Amanda and me, I said, "Yes, we would go." I had heard that if you are asked to do something with the nationals, that you better say Yes, so I did.

    I had also heard that the Banya experience was actually going to a community bath. So, a bath means you do not have clothes on, right? Well, as Amanda and I were getting our things ready, we took along our swimming suits hoping that we could wear them for this experience.

    When we arrived at the Banya, I think we were just taking everything in not knowing what to expect. We entered a space that clearly, we could see that the men and the women were in separate Banyas. Whew, that was good! Next, we went into an area which was kind of like a locker room. I did the "motherly thing" and tried to get Amanda ready first. As I was helping Amanda take off her clothes very slowly, a big Russian lady, fully naked, came bouncing her way over to us. She knew a little English and said something like, it's okay, everybody is naked… just take everything off. Oh no, we were caught. We had to do like the Kazakhstanis do. So, into the Banya fully naked we went.

The next room we walked into was the shower area which was where everyone took their shower. The room was lined with shower heads and was an open space. When they finished their shower, most went into the sauna. In the sauna there were birch branches which people use to beat against the skin. Many countries use birch branches in the sauna to provide relaxation, unclog pores, and to help the skin absorb the essential oils from the birch branches. It also works as an exfoliant to remove dead skin cells. After the sauna, most jump into a very cold swimming pool, still completely naked. It was a rather interesting experience as most Americans are very private and modest and I would have never said that I would agree to such an experience. Then to my surprise, I actually found myself saying "Yes" again when the director asked me to go with her to the Banya a second time.

Christmas With the Boys at Teen Challenge. We had been given "Beanie Babies" from folks in our supporting churches that we took with us to share with children we met. We shared them everywhere we went. We lost count of how many we were given. As Christmas was approaching, David and I were talking about what we could do for the boys. We decided we would buy them stockings, actual heavy-duty stockings (for the harsh winters), stuff one inside the other and then stuff them with all kinds of goodies like we would stuff a Christmas Stocking here in the States for our children. They would receive their very own Christmas Stocking. Then we picked through all the beanie babies we had left and pulled all the animals that we thought the boys would like and gave them an opportunity to pick out whatever beanie baby they wanted. David and I were talking and thinking about the possibility that they would not want a beanie baby, that they would think they were too "babyish." However, they proved that thinking was wrong because every single boy from the age of 5 through 16 including some of the adult boys who were helpers, and the other workers all wanted a beanie baby as their very own. It was so much fun to see their reaction to their gift and we were especially glad to see how they reacted to holding their very own beanie baby.

The building we lived in had a "football" (soccer) field in the back of the building. We could also see snow-capped mountains in the distance year-round. There was a road that went to the soccer field and went past our windows which were at street level. Just beyond our windows there was a fence across the road. People would congregate at that fence outside our windows with loud music, partying, and drinking. Many nights we would pray for them to leave so it would be quiet enough so we could get to sleep.

Prayer Walking. David and I decided we needed to do a prayer walk around the property. We wanted to anoint the grounds and the building for God and for His protection over us. David went to the leadership to ask them about taking a prayer walk, and they were not really interested. So, David and I started anointing the inside areas of our living quarters. We sprayed the walls, the windows and the doors anointing them with oil and praying.

One night we were woken up by banging and crashing sounds. We jumped up to find that the window in our kitchen had been broken. There were people outside our windows who were probably drunk and just horsing around and then they started throwing rocks against the building and windows. Every window in our building had 2 separate windows, an inside window and an outside window. The outside window was broken, but not the inside window, which we had anointed with oil. God showed up and protected us.

Soon after that we had scheduled a trip to meet up with the rest of our missionary team in the northern village of "Sergeyevka." We were going to be away for almost 2 weeks.

As we were preparing to be away, the director came to us and asked us to do a prayer walk and anoint the whole property. David and I, along with some of the leaders, walked around the property and anointed every space that belonged to the boys' home. We anointed the soccer field and claimed the area around the field would flower, and grass would grow. We anointed the building and asked for protection from the enemy that would come against the boys and all the activities on the grounds. We prayed for those that gathered outside our windows. We prayed that they would leave that space and not come back. We anointed that space to be used for God's glory.

The director had 2 rooms which were adjacent to our rooms but were at the very back of the building. She was very scared to be back in that part of the building without us being there.

The first time we visited the village of Sergeyevka, our friend and teammate, Joyce Chellis, David and I went on a prayer walk around the village. As we walked, we prayed for each person that Joyce knew that lived in the houses. We stopped in front of every house where Joyce didn't know the people and prayed for God's blessing on them because God loved them.

As we walked and prayed, we noticed a dog in the distance. We were told that if we saw any wild dogs on our walk that we just needed to leave them alone and walk away from them. But suddenly we realized that the dog was running full force toward us. As he got closer, we saw he was growling, and he was very angry. David said, "Quickly, spray the path in front of us with the oil." So, we sprayed a line straight across the road. And then we stepped back and prayed. That dog ran full force right up to that line... and then suddenly he stopped in his tracks. He turned around and with his tail between his legs, he ran away. God showed up... and HE GLORIFIED HIMSELF.

When we returned from our trip, the director was beside herself with joy and shouting praises to Jesus. The first night we were gone, she was woken up by the loud noises outside our windows. She was very scared, because we were not there... so she began to pray. A few minutes later she heard the one guy shout to the next guy the exact words we had spoken in our prayer... the one guy said, "We have to leave this place - we cannot stay here anymore." The second guy said, "Why, this is a good place to be, we always come here, we like this place." The first guy said, "I don't know why we have to leave, we just have to leave, we cannot stay here." God shows up when we need Him... And HE GLORIFIES HIMSELF.

David worked within the different Teen Challenge programs and led chapel services for the guys. He also became a professor and taught about Worship at the University which was started by Teen Challenge. David also met with individuals one-on-one (along with a translator) to pray with them.

My job was to be an English Teacher because the Teen Challenge Director said that the most important thing needed for those in the Teen Challenge program was for them to learn English. They taught using British English materials; however, he was excited for the folks to hear American English spoken (the director was Australian).

Teen Challenge had these 30 boys, plus all the children of the women and men in their programs, so Teen Challenge started a school. I taught an English class and a Music class in the school. I also taught English in the men's program, at the farm, in the women's program and the refuge program.

Teen Challenge started a church within the different programs as well as in the University they started. Because of David's and my work over 30 years as worship leaders, we worked with the worship teams at all 5 of those churches.

In our first year in Kazakhstan, we found that the people in our churches were singing a lot of hymns and songs that were first translated from English to Russian, and then they were translated from Russian to Kazakh. Some songs were very difficult to translate. David and I wanted to write a worship song that might more easily be translated into Russian and Kazakh. But it was more about writing a worship song than it was about just putting words together that could easily be translated.

In Mark 10:30, Peter says to Jesus… "We have left everything to follow You."

And Jesus responds, "But many who are first will be last and the last first."

For us worship means to Humbly come to the Lord… to Pray to the Lord… and to Bow before the Lord. I believe that this song we wrote, titled, "Humbly" will bless you as you come to the Lord; pray to the Lord; and bow before the Lord.

"Humbly"
by David and Lori Potts
© 2006

Humbly we come to Your house Oh, Lord
Singing a new song to You, singing a hymn of praise
Humbly we come in Your presence Oh, Lord
Bringing our joys and sorrows, laying them at Your feet.

Chorus: Humbly we come… (echo)
Humbly we pray… (echo)
Humbly… we bow before You.

Humbly we pray in Your house Oh, Lord
Lifting our thanks and praises, exalting Your majesty.
Humbly we pray in Your presence Oh, Lord
Our lives are eternally changed, when our time is spent with You.

Chorus: Humbly we come... (echo)
Humbly we pray... (echo)
Humbly... we bow before You.

Humbly we bow before You Lord
Our hearts, a sacrifice, adoring Your Holy Name
Humbly we bow in Your presence Oh, Lord.
On bended knees we come, worshipping at Your throne.

Chorus: Humbly we come... (echo)
Humbly we pray... (echo)
Humbly... we bow before You.

Chorus: Humbly we come... (echo)
Humbly we pray... (echo)
Humbly... we bow before You.

  A Move to Karaganda. We made plans after the first year in Almaty to move to Karaganda where the larger part of our mission family lived and worked. Finally, the day arrived for us to leave Almaty. We ordered a truck that we loaded with our furniture (by this time we had bought beds and "schkofs" (dressers), a dining room table and 4 chairs) to deliver to Karaganda, and we loaded our van with our personal items and left the city of Almaty about 4:00 PM. Our plan was to drive through the night and arrive in Karaganda the next morning. We knew that we would want to have extra petrol (gas) along with us and we were able to purchase 2 cans to fill with petrol to take with us. We also wanted a national friend to ride with us and we chose "Serg" as he did a lot of translation work for us, and David had gotten to know him very well. I expected that David would do most of the driving, so I wasn't particularly worried about anything except for POLICE CHECKPOINTS.
  Shortly after we were on the outskirts of the city, we were stopped at a police check point because they saw David drinking out of a bottle. David drank a lot of lemonade types of drink and was drinking lemonade. When the police were satisfied that it was lemonade, they let us go on our way. The police were known to stop people and give them a fine to pay whenever and for whatever they

wanted. I believe we had to pay a small fine just because they made us stop there.

Just before it started to get dark, I just happened to get out my license and started looking at it. I could not believe my eyes. Somehow, we, I should say I let my PA driver's license expire. It made me very nervous.

Partway through the night we came upon a truck that had jackknifed across the highway. There were no other vehicles or people around, just the truck across the highway and no way around it except to go "off road." So off road we went. I will never forget how completely disoriented we were as we were driving for a long time without seeing any possible way to get back up to the road. It was a little scary, but we had our friend "Serg" with us, and we knew that the Lord was with us, so we continued onward.

After we were back on the road again, at about 1:00 AM, David got very sleepy and asked me to take over driving. I was driving for quite a while when I saw a police checkpoint ahead of me. I came to a stop and looked at the officer. He asked me for my "papers," and I was so afraid of giving him my expired license. I started to get worried and got all flustered that I couldn't find the papers he wanted. It made the officer concerned and he said to "Serg," "What's wrong with her?" "Serg" explained that I was an American and confused and worried about having to stop. The officer was glad to send us on our way without even looking at my papers.

When we arrived at our apartment in Karaganda around 6:00 AM, we found out that our elevator was not working. Our apartment was on the 6th floor. Several of our team members and folks from the church met us around 7:00 AM and helped to carry what we had packed in our van up to our apartment. Our belongings in the truck were not delivered until the following day and the elevator still was not working. So those same folks came back the next day to help carry everything upstairs to our apartment.

One of the first things that was carried up the stairs was our dining room table. They needed to set the table in the hallway outside our door because all the bedroom items, including the bed and dresser, the office items and kitchen items had to be carried through the dining room. When everything was carried in, we went into the hallway to get the table and discovered that our dining room table was not there. We were in total shock. We had to report that it was stolen.

So, over the next few hours there were more police than we ever wanted to see in our apartment, and this was only our second day in Karaganda. They walked outside our door. They took pictures of where the table was and asked all kinds of questions. Fortunately, we had a national lawyer that could deal with those processes, including translation. The documents had to be handwritten a total of 3 times (they had no triplicate forms available). After the police left, we prayed for the person who took our table. We prayed that they would see the face of Jesus on our table. And that if they would return it to us, they could place it outside our door, ring our doorbell and leave. We would not have to know who took our table. Someone placed some notes on our door and the main door downstairs saying the same thing. Then we left the matter with Jesus.

We were exhausted and sat down to relax and grab a bite to eat. When all our helpers left, David and Amanda and I started to unpack some things and put them away when someone rang the doorbell. I ran to the door and looked through the peephole, but I couldn't see anything, it was pretty dark in the hallway. Suddenly both David and I realized that I was actually looking at the top of our table. Someone had returned the table and left it outside our door, rang our doorbell and left. Well, God worked that out.

The apartment buildings in Karaganda mostly had a door in the stairway which opened to 2 or 3 apartments. Our door only had one other apartment. There was an elderly couple who were our neighbors. I rarely talked with the guy. I don't think he wanted to hear my Russian, but the woman and I talked sometimes daily. The woman would make cookies sometimes and share them with us. We followed the custom of never returning an empty dish but made something to share with them when we returned their dish.

One time, she asked me to help her. Her Russian was very hard to understand, but we were able to communicate. She told me that she needed a shot and asked if I could do that for her. I thought to myself, how hard could it be? I had already learned how to give David his insulin shots when he first came home after his toe amputation. Well, let me tell you, it was hard. The next morning, I walked through her door and she handed me a little bottle of the medicine. It looked totally different than any medicine bottle I ever saw here in the States. It had a glass top that needed to be cracked open. I asked her how they open them. She responded by handing me a large kitchen knife, she put the bottle on the table on some folded-up newspaper, and motioned that you whack at it to open the glass. My mind went in all different directions thinking about how the glass would not go into the medicine. I wondered how I was not going to get cut doing this or spill the medicine? But I proceeded. I got the bottle open, drew up the medicine needed, and was prepared to give her shot to her in her arm. She looked at me, turned around, pulled her dress up, and pulled down her underpants. She said the shot goes in the butt. I had to give her a shot in her butt? Well, I had never done that before. I was so hesitant and scared. She motioned to me to just make one fast move to put the needle in and dispense the medicine. I was able to do that, but it was not fun. I am glad that I only had to help her with that medicine for a few days. I did check with our nurse a little later to find out that the glass pieces were a size that would not be able to be pulled into the injection needle. That gave me some relief.

In Kazakhstan and in particular in the city of Karaganda, I was very aware of walking by myself especially after dark. One evening I was at our church helping the worship team. I guess we went a little late, because when I walked out the door it was already starting to get dark. I did have a flashlight with me and our cell phone so I figured I would walk very quickly and get home. As I rounded the corner, I saw a bus at the bus stop and figured I would just follow the people crossing the street from the bus and go across the open land towards our apartment. But there was only one woman, still I thought I would be okay.

But I guess I was walking too slowly, because suddenly I looked up to discover I was not walking behind anyone. I took a quick look over my shoulder and saw a man on the path leading from the opposite corner that would intersect with the path I was on. As I got to the intersection of those two paths, I realized that he was directly behind me. I really didn't think that he was following me, so instead of continuing to go straight ahead, I turned to my left to see if he was really following me and yes, he was. I stopped quickly and he came around to the side of me and spoke to me. I do not remember exactly what I said, but my reaction was to speak in English.

At that point I was more than a little scared, so I turned back and took off running. I ran through the separation of 2 of the buildings and down the walk to the front of my building. I did note something very curious in that usually there are many, many people in the courtyard. Often kids would be playing in the courtyard, and parents would be out with them. There were always young people standing around the cars that were parked and talking. Most of the time there were always "babushkas" (grandmothers) sitting at the front doors of the apartments... but I saw no one.

What was going through my mind was that I didn't want to go into my building. I would have to climb up about 6 or 7 steps, wait at the elevator and possibly he would be able to get in the elevator with me. I did not want that, so I stopped on the porch of my apartment. As soon as I stopped, he grabbed my hand. I remember calling out "Help, me... help me... help me" in Russian as loud as I could. But God was way ahead of me. Immediately a group of about 5 young men came up to me; they circled around me and separated the man from me. One young man said to me where do you live? Interestingly, he spoke to me in English. I said right here. He said go to your apartment.

That whole incident really scared me. I spoke to our field leader that next week and I told him that I saw the guy walking around our courtyard, so he must have been a neighbor. The field leader thought he knew the guy. I explained to the field leader what I did. And, of course, in that moment, I did everything wrong. I spoke to the guy in English, I was carrying a flashlight which the guy probably thought was a bottle of booze and I ran. Well, chalk that up to a learning experience.

All I can say is that it was a moment to learn how God sent those young men even when I don't know where they came from. No one was around; no one was visible as I stood on my porch. They showed up so quickly that I knew God had provided them for me. And I learned that God understood my "Russian."

Maybe I needed to learn to "Fear Not." Maybe, just maybe, you need to learn to "Fear Not." For if you know the Lord, He is right inside you, going through everything right with you.

Over the course of several weeks, David and I wrote several songs. One song was a part of some words that as we tried to put music to the words, actually became two songs: Praise the Lord and Worship the Lord Your God. These are also songs that we thought might be easily translated into Russian and Kazakh.

"Praise the Lord"
by David and Lori Potts
© 2006

Praise the Lord with all of your heart
Praise the Lord with all of your heart
Praise the Lord with all of your heart.
For He is worthy; Exalt His name with every breath.
Praise the Lord with all your heart.

For He is worthy; Exalt His name with every breath.
Praise the Lord with all your heart.

Praise the Lord with all of your mind.
Praise the Lord with all of your mind.
Praise the Lord with all of your mind.
His name is like no other and He... alone is God
Praise the Lord with all your mind.

His name is like no other and He... alone is God
Praise the Lord with all your mind.

Praise the Lord with all of your soul
Praise the Lord with all of your soul
Praise the Lord with all of your soul.
For He is the King of Kings – and He is the Lord of Lords
Praise the Lord with all your soul

For He is the King of Kings – and He is the Lord of Lords
Praise the Lord with all your soul.

"Worship the Lord Your God"
by David and Lori Potts
© 2006

Worship the Lord your God – for He alone is worthy
Worship the Lord your God – for He alone is worthy

Bow before the Lord your God – for He deserves your praises.
Bow before the Lord your God – for He deserves your praises.

Fall facedown before your God – for He has power and He's mighty.
Fall facedown before your God – for He has power and He's mighty.

Worship   *....Worship*
The Lord your God   *....The Lord your God*
For He alone   *....For He alone*
Is Worthy   *....Is Worthy*

Bow before   *....Bow before*
The Lord your God   *....The Lord your God*
For He deserves   *....For He deserves*
Your praises   *....Your praises*

Fall facedown   *....Fall facedown*
Before your God   *....Before your God*
For He has power   *....For He has power*
And He's mighty   *....And He's mighty*

    At one of our mission agency team building conferences, we had this demonstration of the power of names, words, and thoughts.

    We had a young man that stood in front of us. We had been told to think (nothing was spoken out loud) to think about all "GOOD WORDS… ENCOURAGING WORDS… WORDS OF POWER… WORDS OF APPRECIATION…"

    This guy had to pick up a young girl who was sitting on a chair to prove that he was strong... and he did that very well.

    Then they had this same guy stand before us again, but this time we were told to think all negative thoughts (again nothing was spoken out loud) to think negative ideas... words that tore him down… words that said he was weak and powerless… that he couldn't do anything.

    This guy was then asked to do the exact same act of strength that he had just accomplished. However, this time, he was not able to pick up the young girl who was sitting on the chair. He was not able... he was not strong... he was too weak to pick up this young girl… the very thing he had just done earlier.

    I saw this with my very own eyes. Our words and even our thoughts have a powerful effect. Names are very precious and even our thoughts are precious. We can be encouraging to someone with the words we say. I also realize how devastating it can be when we use words that hurt people or put them down.

One time while David was reading scripture, the Lord gave him another song, titled, "My Lord Said, You are so Beautiful." Okay so what about these names: you are not beautiful, you are good for nothin', you will never amount to anything, you are stupid? These days I think these words are often heard. Think about social media and how many times people react to a picture or a thought expressed and respond with negative kinds of words and emojis?

Thank God we don't have to live with those names because God says we are loved, we are beautiful, we are so much more than all those words. He died to save us and to prove His love for us.

Believe it because it is true! God says you are beautiful. You are the one Jesus loves! You are lovable. You are Loved. And we can love others because God loved us first.

"My Lord Said, "You Are So Beautiful"
by David and Lori Potts
© 9/28/2003

My Lord said,
"You are so beautiful," before I was complete in Him
He saw what I could become, when I was so unclean.
I was lost and alone, sinking deep in my sin.
But He gave me joy and freedom that only He could give to me.

My Lord said,
"You are so beautiful; Come with me and let us run"
He knew what I could be if I would only run with him.
I could not see, there was darkness, empty darkness all around.
But then He came and spoke my name, He took my hand and led the way.

My Lord said,
"You are so beautiful; I know a place where we can go."
Only He knows the way, but I must take a step of faith.
He will lead me with His hand – where I've never been before.
It's a narrow way, but wide enough – just wide enough to walk with Him.

Chorus:
My Lord said, "You are so beautiful, come with me and let us run."

My Lord said, "You are so beautiful, come with me and let us run."
My Lord said, "You are so beautiful, come with me and let us run."

When we lived in Karaganda, we were in a very serious car accident. We were almost at the Kazakh Fellowship where we were going to teach on worship. We had just finished praying for our safety, as we always did when we were driving (David was driving and our van was a right-sided drive) when we got to the last major intersection. We had to turn left at a traffic light, and we started to turn. Straight in front of us, a car came out from behind a stopped bus and came straight through the light and hit us on the side of the van. The car was smaller than our van, so the impact flipped our van on its side, and we slid through the intersection right into a car stopped on our left. When our van came to a stop, I heard someone yell, "kick out the windshield," so I did, and we all climbed out of the van basically unharmed. We had been protected but we still went through the accident.

Amanda, was only slightly hurt. She was flipped off her seat because our van only had a lap belt in the back seat. She ended up having several bruises from that. I looked back when the van stopped sliding, and her hand was on the broken window on the road. She lifted her hand, but she only had one small cut. The ambulance showed up and the crew could not believe that they were not needed.

When our friends at the Kazakh Fellowship heard about the accident, they all rushed out to the intersection. Some came to check on us, but then they began to circulate in the crowd. The people were asking a lot of questions, so our friends began to share about what God did. They were able to share the Good News about how God loved them and how God protects those He loves. God showed up... God glorified Himself.

A Move to Segeyevka, Kazakhstan. Over the summer of 2006, the teammate family that lived in the village of Sergeyevka, was back in the States for their 1-year homeland assignment. So, Joyce was by herself in the village. She asked if anyone from the rest of the team in Karaganda would come up to Sergeyevka to spend the summer with her. Of course, David said we would spend the summer in the village.

We loved it in the village. Only 2 roads in and out of the village. I think there was only one stop sign in the entire village and there were no traffic lights. Most of the roads were just dirt roads. There were a couple of "Magazines" (small minute markets, Kazakhstan style) where we could get bread, eggs, water, and cookies, etc. We felt very safe. All the children played outside until supper time, which was around 10:00 or 10:30 PM and then the sun went down shortly after that. This was summertime and there is more daylight than darkness. In winter, it is the opposite. We were in and out of each other's homes often, we didn't do that in the city.

An added blessing while in Sergeyevka, is that there was a private Banya built in the backyard of the house where we were staying. This was a huge difference than the Banya in Almaty. This one was for our private use. Some of the church family had permission to use the Banya, but Amanda and I were always by ourselves using the Banya and David could use it by himself. We were most grateful that we had the Banya experience without having to join everyone else from the city for our bath.

By the end of summer, we started to make plans to return to Karaganda, with the idea of moving to Sergeyevka. However, we did need to renew our visas that fall, and we were hearing rumors that we would be required to leave Kazakhstan to renew our visas, something that none of our teammates had to do. Normally, we would just fill out the proper papers for the renewal and we could do that in Karaganda. We started thinking that we probably would go on vacation to possibly Uzbekistan and renew our visas there. However, when we returned to Karaganda and spoke with our national lawyer about renewing our visas, she said that the requirement was not only that we had to leave Kazakhstan, but we were required to go back to our country of origin. So, we were headed back to the United States to renew our visas. By the time the requirement was sorted out, we only had a couple of days to make the arrangements and get out of Kazakhstan before our visas expired.

We spent about 2- 2 and a half months in the U.S. until our visas were renewed so we could return to Kazakhstan. During that time, my dad celebrated his 80th birthday, and our family was throwing a big birthday party. Earlier I had thought that I wouldn't get to celebrate this milestone birthday with my family as we had no plans to be in the U.S. until the next summer of 2007. I figured being back in the states was not all bad?!? I got to celebrate my father's 80th Birthday with my whole family!

We also had an opportunity to go out to eat with most of David's aunts and uncles, for which I am so thankful that we had that time with them before David's death.

In the later part of October, we purchased 2-way tickets to go to Kazakhstan and then for our return the next year when we would be home on our home assignment. We returned to our apartment in Karaganda and needed to wait until all the paperwork was completed in the city before we could make our plans to move back to Sergeyevka. We arrived in the village around the 12th of November. We were in the village for less than a week, when on Friday, November 17th David passed away.

Chapter Eleven
David Forever with the Lord

> Rejoice always, Pray constantly, Give thanks to God in all circumstances, for this is the will of God in Christ Jesus for you. I Thess. 5:16, 17, 18

I learned this scripture in a song when I was in my youth group. Although, I must admit I had never really understood this scripture.

As I grew up through the years, I would remind myself of this scripture and song. After moving to Kazakhstan, this scripture became very real to me. As I learned about the struggles of the Kazakhstani people and saw how they lived, I reminded them of this scripture to rejoice always. As I saw what little they had and how hard life was for them, I reminded them that scripture tells us to give thanks to God in ALL situations not just when we feel like it; and especially not just when things are going really well.

On that day back in 2006, when my friend, Joyce, our nurse on the field and I realized that David was really gone, we stood, wrapped our arms around each other and cried. I felt my knees go weak and Joyce asked me if I needed to sit down. Just as she said those words, God showed up and I felt His strength flow through my legs, and I knew that I could stand in His strength. We began to pray, and God brought this scripture to my mind. I remember thinking, right now?? Why did you bring this scripture to my mind right now? I can't do this. But I knew that God's Word is true, and I knew that I needed to speak the words. So, I called out to God. I said thank you God. Your Word says to give thanks in all situations. So, I am thanking and praising you, even though it hurts so bad and even though I don't really understand how to do this. Then, He gave me His peace and His comfort, just like He continues to give me these many years later. Amanda said to me right after David passed away that we were going to be okay. And I knew it as I felt God's comfort and peace all around me.

So, we are not to rejoice and give thanks in circumstances just based on the good times in our lives. Scripture says in ALL CIRCUMSTANCES… not just when we choose to. So, if I believe this scripture, and I do; then I better be able to say thanks and be joyful just because of who God is and because of His love. His love for me makes me want to tell others about His love.

We served in Kazakhstan from the summer of 2003 until 2007. In November, 2006, when David passed away, there were two teammates living in the village of Sergeyevka at that time. The larger part of our team was working in the city of Karaganda, an 8 hours' drive away.

On that day, Amanda and I had been out of the house the whole afternoon, and I am so glad that when we returned, she had her friend with her, and they did not go into our bedroom. I was busy putting groceries away and called out a couple of times to David and he did not answer me. So, I went into our bedroom and found him, unresponsive. We always had on and off again phone service, but at that time that I needed to call Joyce to come over, the phone worked. And I also needed to call the rest of the team in Karaganda and tell them. I knew that they would all be together because we always had our English Church on Friday evenings. And again, the phone worked. We arrived home about 5:00 PM. When we spoke with one of the nationals the next day, she said she called on the phone looking for us and David spoke with her around 4:00 PM. She said "What is all this fuss about David not being able to speak Russian. He held a very understandable conversation with her on the phone." David died on Friday, and he was buried on Sunday afternoon as is custom in Kazakhstan. David is buried in the cemetery in the little village of Sergeyevka, Kazakhstan.

A large part of our team in Karaganda drove the 8 hours to Sergeyevka on that Saturday to be with Amanda and me for the funeral. They were there to support us. I remember Saturday evening was especially helpful as our team leaders who were going to do the funeral were helping with the plan. We sat around and discussed songs that we wanted to sing and then we sang them. So just worshipping the Lord that night was so helpful to me.

In our village, many of the believers and the leaders in our church gathered every morning for a time of praise and prayer. While we were there, David and I led that praise time. So, at the meal after the funeral, one of the believers asked me if I was going to be at praise and prayer time the next morning. I didn't even think about my answer, and I said, "YES." She then asked if I was going to lead the singing. I remember thinking and saying, "YES, WHY NOT! WHY WOULDN'T I BE IN WORSHIP AND WHY WOULDN'T I LEAD?"

So, the next morning's praise and prayer time was a very special meeting. We sang so many songs, in English, in Kazakh, and in Russian. It felt to me as if the heavens opened up and we were praising God in all three languages all at the same time. What a sweet, sweet worship time. It was a blessing to be among the believers that gathered that morning. Joyce told me after the prayer time that as we were singing, she saw David singing with the angels in Heaven. No matter what you believe or don't believe about that possibility, I choose to believe that David was singing and praising God and not in any more pain, and no sicknesses.

Documents Translated and Signed by a Notary. In the first couple of days after David passed away, we needed to go to the equivalent of the mayor's office in Sergeyevka to make sure that all our paperwork was in order. That was very difficult as the office workers didn't speak English and between Joyce's and my Russian, we tried to communicate as best we could. You see, they never had a foreigner pass away in their village and they were worried that they would make a mistake. When they were satisfied with the paperwork, they told us that all of David's documents, his passport, his driver's license and the document that showed that he passed away all had to be translated into Russian, and it would only be acceptable if it was translated by a reputable teacher in their eyes. All those documents then needed to be signed by a notary which all had to be done in the village of Atbasar, about a half hour drive away.

We jumped in the car to head to Atbasar in the middle of a snowstorm. Businesses don't advertise there as here in the States, so we really had no idea exactly where to find a notary. Our national friend was with us, and she thought she knew where the teacher was located for the accepted translation. As we reached Atbasar, in the middle of that snowstorm, Joyce was driving, and we were having trouble keeping the windshield clear. She hit the defrost and immediately the car stalled out and wouldn't start again. Our national friend jumped out of the car saying that she was going to go walk to find the expert teacher to get the documents translated.

Well, there we were, Joyce and I just sitting along the road with no heat and in the middle of a snowstorm. Joyce said, "Hey, let's just praise the Lord" and we began to sing our praises to the Lord. It helped us to stay warm and to put our focus on Jesus and not on our situation. As we were singing, Joyce remembered David telling her that there was a button in the car that if it is set, someone would not be able to steal the car because it would not start. Because of the snowstorm, the windows were freezing up so as Joyce hit the defrost, she bumped that button. Joyce hit the button again and the car started so we then had heat. So, as we warmed up, we continued singing praises to the Lord while we waited for our national friend to come back.

Eventually, we saw our friend walking toward us, but she quickly ducked into a little house on the side of the road. After a few minutes, she came to us, jumped into the warm car, and we explained what had happened with the car. Our friend then explained that as she was walking back, she thought she recognized the lady who just happened to cross the street in front of her as the notary.

The amazing thing is that this house, where our car stopped in front of, was the exact place where the notary was located (remember no signs). To top it off, the notary explained that she was not even supposed to be at work this day but that she had forgotten something, so she just stopped into this little house over her lunch hour. When we explained what we needed, she helped us and gave us exactly what we needed. God showed up that day in a very exciting way.

Chapter Twelve
Where Can Worship Take Place?

If you believe in Jesus and have him in your heart, God will always show up. The Lord is always ready and willing to meet you right where you are. Tell him exactly what you are feeling, exactly what you need, and he will meet you because he is ready and willing to meet us exactly where we are.

Someone wants to meet you. The Lord wants to meet you right now. He wants to meet you in the middle of your celebrations. He wants to meet you in the middle of your grief. He wants to meet you in the middle of your discouragement. And He wants to meet you in the middle of your suffering. Call out to the Lord and He will meet you.

The train ride to Karaganda and Psalm 40:3. So, I believe that worship can take place anywhere. But can worship take place on a train? I took a train trip in Kazakhstan with a national friend. I thought it would be fun to sing the songs I knew in Russian and in Kazakh. But it turned out to be a very unique opportunity to play my guitar and sing the songs of my faith in English. My friend played several songs on my guitar and sang in both Kazakh and Russian for several minutes. Then he handed me my guitar and said, "You sing something." When I asked what I should sing and play he answered, "Sing anything you want, just sing in English."

My friend knew that the groups of young men in the train compartments on either side of ours would be very interested in hearing English. So, I began. I was a little apprehensive at first because I didn't want to call attention to myself as an American on that train. But as I sang some songs and worshipped the Lord, I became more confident and shared from my heart. Well, the groups of boys didn't come running over. They didn't even speak to me or my friend. Earlier, their conversations had been very loud, and they were playing card games. But suddenly, their conversations ended, the card games stopped, and they were listening. Remember Psalm 40:3?

"He has put a new song in my mouth, a hymn of praise to our God, many will see and fear and put their trust in the Lord."

Can worship take place in an airport? One time as we were heading home to the States, I was checking through the airport. I always carried my guitar on my back like a backpack, so the officials always asked to check out my guitar. I stepped aside and put my guitar down and opened it. Then the official ran her hands along the guitar and the case inside and outside to do her check. This particular time, the official asked me if I played this guitar. That had never happened before or since. I said, "Yes." So, the official said, "Play it." I remember looking around me at a ton of people. There were other people flying and going through the process, and all kinds of airport workers all around me. I think I swallowed really hard and then went for it. I started playing and singing. I will never know who may have heard or saw me that time, but I worshipped my Lord and Savior, and I know that the Lord can use my worship to lead someone else to put their trust in Jesus. Remember Psalm 40:3?

"He has put a new song in my mouth, a hymn of praise to our God, many will see and fear and put their trust in the Lord."

Chapter Thirteen
New Steps Forward

David passed away on November 17, 2006, a week before Thanksgiving and just 2 weeks before our 23rd Anniversary. Amanda and I headed back to Karaganda by train in time to be with our teammates for our annual Thanksgiving dinner. Amanda stayed at a friend's house, and I stayed with our field leaders and their family. I just couldn't go back to our apartment right away. Our mission agency was working out the details for our "Pastor to the Missionaries" to fly to Karaganda to travel home with us. Finally, the date was scheduled, and we were going to fly out on December 11. We were so fortunate that he came to travel with us. This friend and our field leader went to the airport with us to see us off. I walked up to the checkout desk and handed our tickets (the ones we bought as 2-way tickets for the 3 of us) to the clerk. When the checkout clerk looked at our tickets, she said, "I see Lori and I see Amanda, but where is David?" I remember just staring at her, I didn't begin to know what to say in that moment. Fortunately, both of my friends jumped in, turned me around and pointed me to the seats in the back to sit down. They said, "We got this" and they handled it for me. I didn't have to say the words that David had died. I didn't even have to try. This friend flew the whole way to Philadelphia with us to see that we were okay and connected to my brother and sister who were picking us up and then had another flight back to Atlanta where he lived. I could not have even asked anyone to make that kind of sacrifice of time and effort, but he did it so willingly and we were very grateful.

That week, I met with my pastor at EUM to plan a memorial service for David. It was planned for Sunday afternoon, December 17. Former teammates came from California to be with us and share in the service. Our field leaders also came for support and to share in the memorial service. Of course, we asked Johanna Stahl to share. It was a beautiful service. David's brother sang a couple of songs and our friends from California introduced us to the song, "Blessed Be Your Name" by Matt Redman. They shared that when they worshipped in their church the Sunday after David died, their praise team sang this song. They felt that it was a testament about David's life. It was difficult for me to sing this song at first, but I have come to love it so much! The bridge in the song says, "You give and take away, you give and take away, my heart will choose to say, Lord blessed be your name." When I met with my pastor, I was telling him about the one song that we wrote, "My Lord Said, You are So Beautiful." And the pastor asked me if I would consider singing this song in the Memorial Service. The pastor said that I didn't have to sing, but he thought that I should sing it. I agreed to sing "My Lord Said, You are So Beautiful." My one brother told me after the service that he couldn't believe that I smiled during the service. I told him he was crazy, because I didn't think that I could smile during such a service for my husband. But later, I did see some pictures that someone had taken while I was singing, and I was smiling. That is all to give credit to my Lord and Savior to give me my smile while I praised the Lord.

    The summer after David was with the Lord, Amanda and I were back in the States. My parents were going to be celebrating their 60th Wedding Anniversary on August 15, 2007. I thought it would be a nice present to write a song, so I set out to do so. My sister, Marcia, helped to write some of the words.

    This song is titled, "We Watched How You Loved."

"We Watched How You Loved"
by Lori Potts with Marcia Bollinger
For Richard and Beulah Martin's 60th Wedding Anniversary
© August 15, 2007

We didn't know we had to learn
How to love God and obey His commands
All through the years, every step of the way
You taught us to love as we watched how you love.

When we were young, you showed us love
The kind of love, right from God up above
In work and at play, everyday
You showed us love and taught us to pray.

When we did wrong, you gently would say
It's time to forgive and go back to play
When we obeyed, we knew you were pleased
That big old white house was then filled with peace

With chores in the morning and hard work all day
A trip to "Twin Kiss" is what you would say
We jumped in the car, sometimes in bare feet
We knew that Ice Cream was our special treat

These 60 years, our family has grown
The Lord has been good and we're never alone
You taught us to work and how to have fun
Now it's our turn to do as you've done

Now on this day, this song is for you
We celebrate – the love between two
We want to say thanks and bless you this day
May many more years be coming your way.

And now we know that we had to learn
How to love God and obey His commands
All through the years, every step of the way
You teach us to love as we watch how you love.

    All through David's and my life together, David was the one that always did the writing. He was a pastor and wrote many sermons. He was a student and had to write many papers and he wrote many songs over the years. He also wrote all our newsletters and prayer letters during our missionary time. So, I was now on my own, I had to begin to write our newsletters. I wasn't sure that I could write. I wasn't sure that I could write as well as David. But I began to write our newsletters and prayer letters. Even the song for my parents' 60th Wedding Anniversary, my sister helped me write the words.

    But I just heard that my pastor was going to retire, and I wanted to be able to write a song in his honor. I started praying and asking God about writing a song. Within a few hours in an evening, the following song was written, "Serve the Lord With Gladness" in honor of Pastor Eric and Mary Ritz.

"Serve The Lord With Gladness"
by Lori Potts
In Honor of Pastor Eric and Mary Ritz
© June 10, 2012

We were made to serve the Lord
And Bless His Holy Name
For the Lord is good
His mercies never end
Jesus, He is our Lord!

Serve the Lord with gladness,
Come to Him with Praise
Worship in the house of the Lord.
Serve the Lord with gladness,
Come to Him with Praise
Worship in the house of the Lord

Come into His presence
With thanksgiving
Sing to Him with songs of Praise
For the Lord is good,
His mercies never end
Sing to Him with songs of Praise

Remember that a ship is built
To brave the waves and wind
But when that ship is safe in the harbor
How can that ship fulfill the plan its builders had
The plan to sail from shore to shore

Lord, we thank you for your servants here
Who declare your precious name
And for those who preach your Holy Word
Who proclaim your majesty

We were made to serve the Lord
And Bless His Holy Name
For the Lord is good
His mercies never end
Jesus, He is our Lord!

Soon after Pastor Eric retired, Ray Voran who was our associate pastor announced that he was leaving EUM and moving to New Holland United Methodist Church as their pastor. EUM was planning a farewell luncheon and I so wanted to write another song, this one in Pastor Ray's honor. I prayed about it and opened my Bible and within 2 hours the following song was written. "Proclaim The Truth" based on Isaiah 12:2-6.

"Proclaim the Truth"
by Lori Potts
In Honor of Pastor Ray and Val Voran
© 2012

Proclaim His name from the mountain tops
Proclaim His name from the valley
Proclaim His name day after day
Sing to the Lord and praise His name.
Sing to the Lord and praise His name.

Proclaim the truth… in our words
Proclaim the truth… in our worship
Proclaim the truth… in our lives
He is the way… He is the truth… He is… the life.

The Lord…the Lord is my strength
The Lord… the Lord is my song
With joy we sing of His salvation
I will trust… I will trust… I… will not… be afraid

Give thanks to the Lord and call on His name
Make known what He has done to the nations
Give thanks to the Lord and call on His name
Proclaim His name… Proclaim His name… Exalt… His name.

Sing to the Lord for what He has done
For He has done glorious things
Let His truth be known throughout the nations
Sing for Joy… Sing for Joy… Sing to the… Holy One.

Proclaim His name from the mountain tops
Proclaim His name from the valley
Proclaim His name day after day
Sing to the Lord and praise His name.

Sing to the Lord and praise His name.

David and I had been together in worship and music ministry for almost 30 years. We were a team and did ministry together for so many years. When I first started speaking and sharing about our work in Kazakhstan by myself, it was very difficult without David by my side. But as we were back in the states, I needed to go to our supporting churches to ask them to continue to support us and to also give them time to grieve with me.

I started with a very small church in New Jersey (the church that Pastor Jerry Crossley pastored). Pastor Jerry wanted me to share whatever was on my heart. I remember thinking if, and that was a big if, if I can sing, I will sing, if I can share, I will share, if all that I can do is cry then that is what I will do. I knew that this congregation would be holding me in prayer through it all. I did sing, I did share, and I know that I cried as well. But I knew that it was important for me to share my life with this congregation and the many other congregations that supported our work in Kazakhstan. Each time I shared and sang at these churches, I felt the Lord's presence with me.

Often after I spoke, I would ask the congregation if they had any questions. I remember one person (who happened to know David for many years,) ask openly, "How did David die?" Well, I wasn't prepared for that question in an open church setting, and I wanted to be very careful in choosing the words I would say. It really caught me off guard. I am not sure of my answer but that was the most difficult question to answer, especially in the early days of sharing about David and his death. By the way, the official cause of death was heart failure due to complications with diabetes. This was according to the national nurse in the small village of Sergeyevka that made the determination based on what we had said about David.

I don't speak in churches like that anymore. I am not receiving any support from any of those churches. But I do rely on God's direction in sharing stories as I am in conversations. I tell of God's faithfulness, God's protection, and God's love. I look for opportunities in my church to share stories of God's faithfulness. I look for opportunities at my work (church) to share stories of God's goodness. I look for opportunities in my conversations to point people to Jesus. I am most certain that I need to be sharing my story and singing my praise to the Lord.

Back in 2014-2015 when I found I was without a job for over a year, I was really struggling. I ended up meeting with several people at EUM for accountability as the church was helping me with my rent. When folks from this accountability group asked me why I didn't get a job yet or why I can't find a job, I would say I didn't know and that I was doing all I knew to do. I would apply to places and then never hear anything back from them. I had no calls for interviews. I just would not hear anything from them. It was so disappointing, and I was really trying to trust God. I doubted God's faithfulness in my life, and I didn't like that. But I knew deep down in my heart that God was still faithful, and that I needed to continue to trust that He was faithful. I found that I needed to do something physical to show my trust and not just say the words. So, I found that if I put my hands out in front of me, palm side up, and say I trust you Lord, I could sense God's peace and His encouragement in my soul. When I felt discouraged, I would say to myself, I trust you, Lord and put my hands out in front of me. When I applied to places and never heard anything back from them, I would say to myself, I trust you, Lord and throw my hands out in front of me. Sometimes, all I could do was to throw my hands out and not even say the words. Sometimes, I couldn't say the words because I was crying, so doing something physical helped me say the words without speaking the words. Sometimes Amanda reminded me of trusting in the Lord by putting her hands out in front of her and not saying a word. I so needed those reminders of trusting the Lord over and over again.

In early July 2015, I saw an ad that Millersville Community Church needed a Church Secretary. I applied on a Friday, the day before July 4th, so I figured it might be a while until I would hear from them. But I got a phone call the following Monday to set a time for an interview and I began working at Millersville Community Church on July 20. It happened that fast!

When I interviewed, I met with the previous pastor and a church administrator. I felt that the interview went very well. When I stood up to leave, the pastor said that we needed to take care of part 2 of the interview. I didn't know anything about a part 2 of the interview. He took me to the church secretary's office. I was asked to sit down at the computer, and I was handed a couple of papers with some information. I was told to create a folder in a certain place on the computer, create a press release and a flyer for an event that was listed on the papers they handed me. I was given a website to grab a graphic to go with the flyer I was to create. I had to save what I created in that folder. I was given all the details, but I had to create the press release and flyer using Publisher. I had to save it under a folder I created for myself on the computer and all within 20 minutes. At the same time, there was a meeting going on in the room next to where I was so there was noise coming from that room. There were 2 people sitting in the same room I was in, and they were talking. And as the pastor left the room, he said let's just keep the door open, so she knows what it is like around here with all the noise and commotion of people. Phew! I had my work cut out for me. I tried not to let the 20 minutes rattle me. After I was hired and going through the training, I was told that I was the only one that completed every detail of the assignment. I am so thankful for my job that I still have with Millersville Community Church, but now as Church Secretary, Church Administrator and Coordinator for the Facilities and Church Calendar.

In early 2016, our worship leader, Kelly Saylor, at EUM announced that her family was moving to Delaware. She was leaving as our worship leader. I decided I wanted to write a worship song in her honor, so I prayed and "Forever Sing… Praise to the Lord was written.

"Forever Sing… Praise to the Lord"
by Lori Potts
In Honor of Kelly Saylor, Worship Leader at EUMC
  © April, 2016

Praise to the Lord!
Praise to the Lord!
Forever sing… forever sing,
Praise to the Lord!

There is joy in the Lord,
when we sing His praises.
For He alone, deserves our praise.
Come let us sing, praise to the Lord!

There is peace in the Lord,
when we put our faith… in Christ Jesus.
Lift up your face, look in His eyes.

Fall back and rest in His loving arms!

There is love in the Lord,
because He loved before we could.
He showed us how… to walk this life.
And now we live as He would live!

There is victory in the Lord,
when we call the name of Jesus.
Come to the Lord, give Him your heart.
Forever sing, Praise to the Lord!

Praise to the Lord!
Praise to the Lord!
Forever sing… forever sing,
Praise to the Lord!

In the fall of 2016, my niece Jenni was planning her wedding. She asked me to sing a song for her wedding and she wanted it to be a part of the "Cord Ceremony" using the scripture that when 2 or 3 cords are woven together, they are stronger than one cord alone. When I asked if there was a special song she wanted, she said "Bind Us Together." I love that song, but decided I was going to write my own song, and I entitled it, "Bind Us Together." I surprised her with her own special wedding song.

"Bind Us Together"
by Lori Potts
In Honor of
Jennifer Bollinger and Douglas Weidman's Wedding
© September 24, 2016

It takes three to love the way God loves you
It takes three to discover the way
It takes three to make your marriage strong
It takes three to live as man & wife.

The gold cord stands for God and His glory.
The purple cord stands for the groom

The white cord stands for the bride
Now weave them into one

This is the way to show your love
Take the three cords and make it one
Just as these cords are woven together
God will bind you together in love

This is your day to show your love
Before God, your family and friends
To give your life and hearts to each other
Remember His great love for you

Look at the cords as they're woven together
It's much stronger than one cord alone
When you choose to love as God loves you
He will bind you together in love.

It takes three to love the way God loves you
It takes three to discover the way
It takes three to make your marriage strong
It takes three to live as man & wife.

Chapter Fourteen
Talk About Steps Forward?

The Story of Lori & Carl. One man from that accountability group at EUM, along with his small group had recently started a group for widows and widowers called "Going Forward" which met monthly for a covered dish dinner and some type of entertainment or speaker. Rather than a grief help group, it was started to "take the next step." It was started to find ways of meeting others in the same situation and to support each other with friendship and activities. This man said that I should come to "Going Forward." I had heard of "Going Forward" before this, but I knew I would be the youngest person there. I was only 46 when David passed away. Why would I go? Most people were a lot older than me. But this man asked me to be one of the leaders by being in charge of the kitchen, by helping with the food set up, making coffee and also being the group's secretary. I finally agreed and started attending. It was just like I figured it would be. I was the youngest person there.

I had gone to "Going Forward" for a couple of months when I got a phone call from Carl Zimmerman asking me out on a date. He said he had met me at "Going Forward." To me, the phone call and the request for a date were quite out of the blue. I was blown away. It was now over ten years since David passed away. I had not been on any dates and was never asked out by anyone. I kind of figured that I would not ever meet anyone to love again.

I put Carl off for a little while, at least until "Going Forward" met the next month. Then I said, "Yes" I would go out on a date."

Carl's side of the story is that he attended "Going Forward" for a couple of months after his wife had recently passed away. He was looking for a helpmate. He had decided that he would not continue to come, except that this month, I had started coming and he met me. He really pursued me and his love for me captured my heart.

I believe that people who have been single for too long are the hardest to find love again. They've become so used to being single, independent and self-sufficient that it takes someone extraordinary to convince them that they can love and be loved again.

I had been single for 10 years and pretty much felt that there was no one else for me. Not one date, not one phone call, not one indication that anyone was interested in me. I felt that I was that person who would be single for the rest of my life. David and I had a wonderful relationship, and I loved him dearly. He knew me better than I knew myself. I knew that it would take someone extraordinary to convince me that they were needed in my life. I believe that to be Carl and I said "Yes" to become his wife. I told Carl that we needed to tell my parents. So, to the care facility we went to tell mom and dad. I thought we would just tell them, but Carl got down on his knee and asked me to marry him in front of my parents. I have a very special picture in my mind of my mom clapping when she heard those words. Mom didn't live to attend our wedding, but that picture of her clapping at the news of our marriage has carried me through.

    Writing "Another Bump in the Road." As I shared quite often at "Going Forward" about some of the songs that I had written, Carl asked me if I ever wrote a song using just a simple phrase. I said no that I hadn't. So, Carl said, "See if you can write a song using the words, "Another Bump in the Road."

"Another Bump in the Road"
by Lori Potts
© Summer 2016

But what if those bumps help us turn our hearts to Jesus Christ.
And then we trust in Him to help us through each day.
Receive the gift of Grace He freely gives to you.
And let Him smooth the bumps in your road of life.

He never promised us green pastures.
Somehow the dust and dirt of life get in the way.
When I can't give my troubles to the Master
It's just another bump in the road of life.

He doesn't promise blue skies without gray
The clouds roll in and the sadness fills my heart
When my circumstances make it very hard to pray
It's just another bump in the road of life.

He never promised sunshine without rain.
The sun does not always shine
When tears fall and my heart is full of pain
It's just another bump in the road of life.

But what if those bumps help us turn our hearts to Jesus Christ.
And then we trust in Him to help us through each day.
Receive the gift of Grace He freely gives to you.
And let Him smooth the bumps in your road of life.

    As you can imagine this was a difficult time for Amanda as she grew up from the age of 12 with only her mother. We had a wonderful relationship, and we did practically everything together. And now, there was someone else in my life.

    About a month before the wedding, Amanda was helping me decide what jewelry to wear with my wedding dress and we were talking. She asked me if I wanted her to walk me down the aisle? I was excited and said, "Yes I do." A few days later she asked me again if I wanted her to walk me down the aisle? I said, "Yes, I am counting on it." With much prayer and many, many conversations, she was able to walk me down the aisle to marry Carl. Carl and I were married on January 20, 2018.

    Carl became my best friend, the one I could turn to for support, to laugh with me, and to love for always and forever. He became that extraordinary someone in my life. I decided I wanted to write a song for our wedding, and I wanted to surprise Carl by singing at our wedding. So, I even snuck my guitar to the church, asked a friend to be sure it was where I needed it to be and to tune it for me, so it was ready to go in the ceremony at the right time. I believe I indeed surprised Carl with this song, "Two Lives…Two Hearts."

"Two Lives…Two Hearts"
by Lori Potts
For My Wedding to Carl Zimmerman
© on January 20, 2018

Two lives…two hearts, standing together in Love
Our lives…our hearts, united by the Author of Love

Today we come
We stand before you now
We choose to love and make our solemn vow
We ask you, Lord.
To weave our hearts into one

And add your strength to keep us faithful to you

And as I stand
I give you all my love
And thank you for patiently waiting for me.
So, take my hand
Let's walk the road God planned for us,
To love and care and cherish throughout our lives

Lord, by Your grace
Fulfill your love in us
That we might serve faithfully in your world
Now bless us Lord
Establish our home in peace and love
So, we might show
The love you gave to us.

Two lives…two hearts, standing together in Love
Our lives…our hearts, united by the Author of Love

    The Story of Amanda and Andrew. As Carl and I were dating, Amanda met Andrew Troutman at work. They began to date. Soon she announced to me that he was the "ONE" for her. Even before she began dating, I had talked about giving her daddy's wedding ring to her. As we talked, I decided I would give her all of our wedding rings. They got my diamond ring re-set for her and then they took both David's and my wedding rings and made one ring for her, so she has both her mother's and father's wedding rings as her wedding ring. That was very important to her, and I felt it was the best gift I could give her.

    On October 17, 2020, Amanda Potts married Andrew Troutman in a private wedding in Amanda's backyard. Following their wedding they opened their backyard and received the extended family at a reception. They had initially planned the wedding and reception at another venue, but this was 2020 (the year of COVID) and plans changed so rapidly. Finally, Amanda said to me, let's just have a very private wedding with me, Andrew's parents and his sister, and then invite the extended family to the reception. Amanda asked our former field leader from Kazakhstan who is now in Georgia to perform her ceremony. This was very special as we had not seen him and his wife for many years. It was very special as our field leader performed David's funeral and I spent many days living with his family in Karaganda after David passed away. Having them be a part of this wedding was so comforting. I planned to secretly write a song for their wedding, and I sang "A Love So Strong" at their wedding.

"A Love So Strong"
by Lori Zimmerman © 2020
Song for Amanda and Andrew's Wedding
October 17, 2020

There is such great love…. A mother has for her child
There is such great love…. A bride has for her groom
There is such great love…. A groom has for his bride
There is such great love…. Jesus died to show His love

But the only way to love…. Is to learn
Jesus loved you first
He loves you best. His love goes ever strong!
Jesus loved you first,
He loves you best. His love goes ever strong!

(to: Amanda)
As I held you in my arms: I caught your first smile.
I remember how your daddy held you like a baby doll on his knee.
Now I see you standing here…. the young lady you've become.
So let me tell you dear…..my love keeps going strong.

(to: Andrew)
When I first heard your name and learned to know you.
I saw your kindness and your gentleness and the way that you smiled.
When I learned how much she loves you as she gave you her heart.
Please promise all your love…. and never let her go.

(to: Amanda & Andrew)
Now you stand here in this place… to pledge all your love
And give the rings to show…. your un-ending love

When the preacher says the words of love and says you're man & wife.
Then your love.... can keep on going strong.

When Jesus says He loves you, he waits for you to say.
That you'll love him too and try to... follow in his way.
When the road is long and difficult, always choose to love
For His love for you... will keep on going strong.

There is such great love.... A mother has for her child
There is such great love.... A bride has for her groom
There is such great love.... A groom has for his bride
There is such great love.... Jesus died to show His love

And now the family tree goes on... my granddaughter, Brielle Faith Troutman was born to mom & dad, Amanda and Andrew on June 22, 2024. Amanda wanted me to be with her through the whole birth (from inducing to birth). It was awesome to see Brielle being born. She is so special! It is wonderful watching her meet and exceed the milestones in her life. She is 9 months old as of this writing. Recently, she was caught in a photo of her eyes closed and her hand up high in praise to Jesus! Her newest fete is to take one step forward using a children's walking toy. I pray that she will take her steps with Jesus one step at a time, just as she is learning to walk, one step at a time!

Chapter Fifteen
Closing
God Shows Up and Glorifies Himself

God shows up… And HE GLORIFIES HIMSELF. God created each of us to glorify Him through loving those around us. The more we love God, the more we reflect His loving image back to those around us.

I truly believe that God cares more about our willingness and our being available than about the things that we are able to do, even though He gives us those abilities. We must be willing and available no matter what He is asking us to do, where He is asking us to go, or what we may have to endure along the way. Are you willing? Are you available? When we become willing and make ourselves available, God gives us joy. And He doesn't stop there. He also gives us the knowledge and the strength to do exactly what he has called us to do.

God loves you and me so much! Think about it. The creator of everything is our loving Heavenly Father and He wants us to love Him. Although I deserve punishment for my selfish choices, God chose His Son to take that punishment and die for me; God chose His Son to die for all of us. He chose for us to live forever with Him. He longs for us to love Him and trust Him. We need to trust in the Lord so that we don't follow our own selfish desires.

The Bible tells us to let the Holy Spirit fill and control us. This means that we are so filled with the light of the Lord that the Lord transforms our behavior – the Lord transforms all we say and do. When we allow the Holy Spirit to control our lives, our life will be like beautiful music.

So, I will shout His name. I will sing His praises. I will cry out so the stones will not have to burst into cheers.

> "And he answered and said unto them, I tell you that, if these should hold their peace, the stones would immediately cry out." Luke 19:40 (KJV)

The words from a favorite song titled, "How Can I Keep from Singing" by Chris Tomlin, Ed Cash, and Matt Redman say it this way,

"I am loved by the King and it makes my heart want to sing."

How can I keep from singing the Lord's praises, when He has done so much for me? Many times, I sing because I want to. Sometimes I sing because I am asked to sing, but there are times when I just don't feel like singing praises. I don't feel like praising God. I don't feel like shouting, "Praise the Lord." But those are the times, that I must praise the Lord. I must shout, "Praise God" for in those moments is when I show my obedience to rejoice always, pray constantly, and give thanks to God in all circumstances.

I hope that in the reading of this book and my story that you see God's hand in my life leading me one step at a time. If you know Jesus as your Lord and Savior, I pray that your heart is encouraged to see his hand in your life too. If you do not know Jesus, I pray that you will come to know God who loves you, comforts you no matter what you are going through, gives you direction and heals you. Maybe today is the day that you call upon Jesus to come into your life and guide you to be the person He created you to be. Simply call out to Jesus and he will come into your life. As I think about my life, I see his love for you even as I write my story.

I am most grateful to God for this my story. I am thankful for His direction, care and love in my life. I am thankful for giving me my family, for giving me my husband, David, for my daughter, Amanda and her husband, Andrew, and now my new husband, Carl. And for the newest person in my life, my grandbaby, Brielle.

I am grateful to Amanda who walked through part of this story with me. I am grateful to my husband, Carl, who came along to journey through this life with me. And I am most grateful for my parents and siblings; this family that God gave me.

I am grateful for all the friends that I have and have had over the years. Some have come and gone in my life, some have never left, and some I don't see very often, but every time we get together, it is as though we never were apart. I attribute that to the fact that these are my sisters in Christ, that makes them just the most special friends to have.

I am also grateful to many pastors who I have as friends. One pastor, Pastor Jerry Crossley and his wife, Julie have been most encouraging to me over many years and encouraged me in the writing of this book. I probably never would have written anything. However, in the process of writing these stories, I am reminded that it has all been a part of God's work in my life. It has all been a part of God taking me one step(pe) at a time.

Another Pastor is Pastor Kerry Leeper from Millersville Community Church where I work. Pastor Kerry is my pastor, my boss, my co-worker, my friend, and my partner in ministry. Countless conversations have given me opportunities to speak of the Lord's goodness in my life and to tell my stories of God's faithfulness.

Another Pastor is Pastor Ray Voran from Friendship Church in New Holland, my pastor where I am a member and lead the praise team to usher people into worship. Pastor Ray is the associate pastor who left EUM Church to become pastor at New Holland United Methodist Church in whose honor I wrote the song, "Proclaim the Truth."

Recently, EUM Church and New Holland United Methodist Church have merged to become Friendship Church in New Holland. And I am most grateful that I get to call Millersville Community Church and Friendship Church my church families.

When I think back at that moment when I asked God if I was to get rid of all my belongings to be able to move to Kazakhstan, I didn't really hear an answer. However, I knew at that moment that God was taking me one step at a time through this journey of my life. When I have taken one step, then another step, and then many steps, and I look back at my journey, I can say with all certainty that God was walking with me one step(pe) at a time. And I need to give the Lord all praise for how and when and why and where he worked in my life.

Sometimes I ask, "Who Am I?" that the Lord has been so good to me and has been that guide in my life that I can count on? Well, I do know who I am. I am the Lord's chosen, the Lord's daughter, and the Lord's beloved. I am most certain that this love that the Lord has for me, he has for everyone. And his love for me compels me to sing. And I will sing Humbly, I Come Into Your House, Humbly, I Pray In Your House, and Humbly I Bow Before You Lord!

Reprise of the song, HUMBLY!

"Humbly"
by David and Lori Potts
© 2006

Humbly we come… (echo)

Humbly we pray... (echo)
Humbly... we bow before You.

Humbly we come to Your house Oh, Lord
Singing a new song to You, singing a hymn of praise
Humbly we come in Your presence Oh, Lord
Bringing our joys and sorrows, laying them at Your feet.

Chorus: *Humbly we come... (echo)*
Humbly we pray... (echo)
Humbly... we bow before You.

Humbly we pray in Your house Oh, Lord
Lifting our thanks and praises, exalting Your majesty.
Humbly we pray in Your presence Oh, Lord
Our lives are eternally changed, when our time is spent with You.

Chorus: *Humbly we come... (echo)*
Humbly we pray... (echo)
Humbly... we bow before You.

Humbly we bow before You Lord
Our hearts, a sacrifice, adoring Your Holy Name
Humbly we bow in Your presence Oh, Lord.
On bended knees we come, worshipping at Your throne.

Chorus: *Humbly we come... (echo)*
Humbly we pray... (echo)
Humbly... we bow before You.

Chorus: *Humbly we come... (echo)*
Humbly we pray... (echo)
Humbly... we bow before You.

List of Original Songs

Gave Me You: a Song for Lori	Page 37
Humbly	Page 69
Praise the Lord	Page 74
Worship the Lord Your God	Page 75
My Lord Said, "You Are So Beautiful"	Page 77
We Watched How You Love In Honor of Mom and Dad's 60th Anniversary	Page 88
Serve the Lord With Gladness *In Honor of Pastor Eric and Mary Ritz*	Page 89
Proclaim The Truth *In Honor of Pastor Ray and Val Voran*	Page 91
Forever Sing... Praise to the Lord *In Honor of Kelly Saylor*	Page 94
Bind Us Together *In Honor of Jennifer and Douglas Weidman's Wedding*	Page 95
Another Bump in the Road	Page 98
Two Lives... Two Hearts *In Honor of My Wedding to Carl*	Page 99
A Love So Strong *In Honor of Amanda and Andrew Troutman's Wedding*	Page 101
Humbly - Reprise	Page 105

Other titles from Higher Ground Books & Media:

Wise Up to Rise Up by Rebecca Benston

It's Only a Game by Darrel Johnson

Our Journey of Faith by Miranda Thornsberry

People in Our Lives by Henryk Hoffmann & Friends

Raven Transcending Fear by Terri Kozlowski

The Power of Knowing by Jean Walters

Journey to the Mountaintop by Terra Kern

Through the Sliver of a Frosted Window by Robin Melet

Music & the Holy Spirit by Stephen Shepherd

Full Gospel by Rev. Jerry C. Crossley

The Real Prison Diaries by Judy Frisby

Shameless Persistence by Sandra Bretting

Add these titles to your collection today!

http://www.highergroundbooksandmedia.com

HIGHER GROUND BOOKS & MEDIA IS AN INDEPENDENT PUBLISHER

Do you have a story to tell?

Higher Ground Books & Media is an independent Christian-based publisher specializing in stories of triumph! Our purpose is to empower, inspire, and educate through the sharing of personal experiences. We are always looking for great, new stories to add to our collection. If you're looking for a publisher, get in touch with us today!

Please be sure to visit our website for our submission guidelines.

http://www.highergroundbooksandmedia.com/submission-guidelines

HGBM SERVICES IS OUR CONSULTING FIRM

AUTHOR SERVICES

HGBM Services offers a variety of writing and coaching services for aspiring authors! We can help with editing, manuscript critiques, self-publishing, and much more! Get in touch today to see how we can help you make your dream of becoming an author a reality!

*****

We also offer social media marketing services for authors, small businesses, and non-profit organizations. Let us help you get the word out about your book, your projects, and your mission. We offer great rates, quality promos, consistent communication, and a personal touch!

http://www.highergroundbooksandmedia.com/editing-writing-services

Need Bulk Copies?

If you would like to order bulk copies of this book or any other title at Higher Ground Books & Media, please contact us at highergroundbooksandmedia@gmail.com.

We offer discounts for purchases of 20 or more copies. Excellent for small groups, book clubs, classrooms, etc.

Get in touch today and get a set of great stories for your students or group members.

www.ingramcontent.com/pod-product-compliance
Lightning Source LLC
Chambersburg PA
CBHW060844050426
42453CB00008B/824